PS374.N4T5

TISCHLER
BLACK MASKS

DATE DUE

DATE D			
MAY 9 1973			
APR 23			
MAY 2 '90			
DEC 16 '02			

DATE DUE

BLACK MASKS

NEGRO CHARACTERS IN

MODERN SOUTHERN FICTION

Nancy M. Tischler

The Pennsylvania State University Press
University Park and London

Standard Book Number 271-00082-1

Library of Congress Catalogue Card 68-8187

Printed in the United States of America

to my mother-in-law, Edith Tischler,

in gratitude for her generosity and love

CONTENTS

BLACK MASKS

1

TYPES, STEREOTYPES, AND ARCHETYPES

"We wear the mask," says Laurence Dunbar, "that grins and lies, / It hides our cheeks and shades our eyes,—." This mask of comedy, labeled over seventy years ago by the poet, has often covered the face of tragedy. The artist has followed societal patterns by accepting the truth of the mask itself during the early years of our century, gradually learning to perceive a diversity of masks, then a hint of another truth behind the masks, and finally to doubt that the truth lies in the mask at all. In more recent days, the artist has been inclined to wonder whether the mask is a total lie, or whether it may have some effect on the man beneath it if he wears it too long—like Pirandello's hero who plays mad so long that he becomes mad. The current cliche is that there is no such thing as The Negro, that Negroes are as disparate as any other group of humans and may not be neatly categorized. But the Black Nationalists, among others, insist that there is a unique Negro experience which the race shares and which draws its members together.

Whether or not there are Negro types in life, there certainly are in art, which is our stylized vision of life. Man's automatic response to the diversity of human nature is classification. The consequent simplification does some violence to individuality, which the modern finds so precious, but has compensations in the resulting universality. Typing has always been one of the most useful of artistic tools, and one of the most dangerous in the hands of the unskilled. It is the typing of the pilgrims in Chaucer's Prologue that delights and informs us. Nor do we feel that by characterizing his pilgrims as pardoners, innkeepers, knights, squires, yeomen, or wives, Chaucer eliminates their individual humanity. Their gap teeth, their hairy nostrils, their modes of wiping gravy from their chins fix them in our imaginations as real people.

Authors have found that the type is, in the long run, the key to allying their characters to the collective psyche; when the character acts out the race's rituals, then he is in touch with archetypal patterns. Obviously, to construct characters with a deliberate effort to produce archetypes can result in ridiculous, inartistic, or pretentious creations. The archetypal pattern alone no more insures the novel's immortality than does its absence assure the novel's evanescence.

For the Southern artist, the problem of balancing the type against the individual is most acute when dealing with Negro characters. And the Southern writer has very little choice—if he is to write about the South, he must write about the Negro. Negroes are an inescapable part of Southern life, confronting the white man from birth to death, present for the ecstatic and mundane parts of human existence. Living in an intimate relationship with the white man, the Negro often remains an enigma to the very people who see him daily and who accept him as an essential component of their lives. Paradoxically, the social situation in the South which has made the Negro a mystery to the white man has given the Negro a vast and precise knowledge of the white Southerner. Nat Turner in Styron's novel notices that Negroes often have very private knowledge of white activity, sharing secrets that occasionally make whites nervous and cruel toward the black Tiresiases. One of the earliest scholarly commentators on the Southern Negro, Howard Odum, suggests that whites can never know the Negro because he does not exist as a single personality: Each Negro is, in fact, four people— "what he is, what the white man thinks he is, and what he might be and what he desires to become."[1] Others have speculated along the lines that Pirandello pursues—that no man has a consistent personality or one that art can honestly reproduce. Not simply four personalities, most of us have a new personality for each moment in time and for each person we meet. If we accept the concept of the fluid personality, we find any effort to fix character in art ludicrous and dishonest. And it is patently fatuous to attempt to define not simply one person but a whole race.

On such a sandy foundation, the artist must construct his clearly shaky artifice out of the stuff of his experience and his imagination. And here again, the Southern artist finds himself in a curious position. Because of the severely circumscribed role the Negro plays in Southern life, he seldom appears to the white man as clearly individual. Traditionally a hewer of wood and a drawer of water, he even now appears most consistently only in the most menial of roles: as the house servant, the mammy, the yard man, the porter, the bellhop, or the share-cropper.

Southern white men and women have had little occasion for intimate and prolonged contact with Negro profession-al people. Even today it is considered improper or worse for a white man to invite a Negro to be a guest in his home, although he may visit in a Negro home with impunity. Story after story shows the Negro friend entering by way of the back door, feeling ill at ease in the living room, preferring that the white man come to his home instead. And a number of writers also picture the discomfort of such a return visit: the honking of the horn so the Negro will come outside for conversation, the sense of strangeness if one enters the Negro house, the surprise if the furnishings are not typically Negro.

In addition, few Southerners would have first-hand knowledge of the "new Negro" as a type. The number of doctors, lawyers, teachers, and ministers among Southern Negroes has remained relatively small inasmuch as the talented Negro is sorely tempted to move North, although recently there has been a softening of attitudes in the South that has lured a few educated Negroes back to the area they still consider home. While the new Negro was a topic of excited discussion in the North by the 'twenties, he has been evident in the South only in the last two decades.

The Southern Negro, then, has been known largely in his role of servant, a role which demands certain stereo-typed responses. Several more perceptive authors have seen through the role-playing of the Negro servant and por-trayed the character within the stereotype. For example, in one of the first of the new Negro-centered Southern novels—*Birthright*—T.S. Stribling laughed at the common portrayal of the Negro servant. In a particularly painful scene, the hero (an educated young mulatto) has been hired as a companion by a white "aristocrat," who is apparently the mulatto's father. In his anger at being forced to serve a white man in spite of his education and in lieu of his grandiose dreams of setting up a school for Negroes, the boy parodies his own role. His bowing and scraping are so outrageous that they infuriate his employer-father. In Stribling's use of the scene, we find an unusually acute awareness of the feelings of the man behind the faithful-servant mask. Robert Penn Warren, William Styron, and William Faulkner are among a number of moderns who have commented on this grotesque role the Southerner has demanded of his Negro servant and on the effect that the role-playing must eventually have on the man wearing the mask.

Even when the Negro is not a servant, the Southerner has often expected him to play the role of "nigger"—that is to accommodate his response to the expectations of the white man. A Negro walking down the street may find himself accosted as "boy" and be asked to deliver a message in return for a dime—even if that Negro is a doctor, venerated by his people and well-thought of in white circles. Faulkner's stories of Lucas Beauchamp and his rejection of the "nigger" role are, of course, the outstanding studies of this pattern of Southern life. Dunbar says that the "mask that grins and lies" is the "debt we pay to human guile." Demanding the mask-appearance in society has often blocked the white author from intimate knowledge of the Negro's character, mind, or tastes.

There are also other problems that make it almost impossible for the Southern white man to understand the Negro: The Southern Negro is most often non-verbal, frequently illiterate, usually much poorer than the whites of the community. He is therefore almost completely incomprehensible to the middle or upper-class, literate, verbally oriented white author. Lacking any contrary information, the middle-class white man may therefore accept without question the prevailing social and cultural stereotypes of the Negro and incorporate them into his novels. Even Negro critics and writers admit that some of the old stereotypes were not entirely without foundation. Sterling Brown confessed that "individuals could be found resembling Page's Uncle Billy or Stark Young's William Veal or Dixon's brutal Gus, or Scarlet Sister Mary or Van

Vechten's Lasca, or even Uncle Tom or Florian Slappey."[2] When there is some initial truth for the stereotype and when the people involved continue to play the stereotyped role, it is hardly remarkable that stereotypes have persisted so long as they have.

It is always a temptation to stereotype the unfamiliar since the writer must rely on hearsay, popular ideas, reading, and imagination to produce his characters. This explains Defoe's Friday as well as many of the stereotyped aristocrats and poor whites in Southern fiction. And to this we must add Sterling Brown's assertion that the majority most often stereotype racial and minority groups.[3] This tendency is apparent in the English stereotypes of Irish and Scots and our stereotypes of Italians and Orientals as well as of Negroes.

If the writer must penetrate these multiple barriers of role-playing and bridge the social, educational, and psychological gaps separating him from his black neighbors, as well as overcome the human temptation to categorize the unfamiliar, it is remarkable that so many white Southerners have worked with Negro-oriented novels. But only a handful have attempted stream-of-consciousness techniques, deep psychological probing, or an exclusively Negro point-of-view. Notice that it is a standard critical commentary on *The Sound and the Fury* that Faulkner fails to give Dilsey a stream-of-consciousness section parallel with that of each of the other main characters. Apparently he felt incapable of putting himself in the place of the Negro, although he chanced identifying with a woman and an idiot—a striking commentary on his belief in the remoteness of Negro psychology. And one of the most typical criticisms of Styron's *The Confessions of Nat Turner* has been that he dared, with dubious success, tell the tale as a first-person narrative.

Yet, in spite of all these preliminary difficulties, the presses have been flooded with Negro-centered books by Southerners. Some years back Odum cited 5,000 full-sized books on the Negro by Southerners, of which one-half are "literature," 1,000 are volumes of fiction, 500 are biography, 400 are poetry, and 125 are drama. In addition, there are 800 volumes of history, 800 studies of Negro life, 400 on nature and folk, and 100 on each of socio-economic studies, nature and resources, and travel and description.[4] John M. Bradbury gave over an entire chapter in his *Renaissance in the South* to recent books on the Negro, citing a vast number as worthy of critical acclaim. Obviously, a large proportion of the books are failures for various reasons, one of the main ones being the intellectual arrogance of the man of limited intelligence who thinks his superficial knowledge of one small group of Negroes in a certain area justifies his claim to be a knowledgeable specialist on "The Negro." Many of the novels fail because of obvious exploitation of sensationalism, violence, and sex; or their author's excessive sincerity results in cardboard characters and contrived situations.

Even those authors who have eventually produced good Negro-centered novels and stories have not been uniformly successful. In the case of Faulkner's uneven pattern, Irving Howe sees the path as a progression from stereotype to deep psychological probing. And Seymour Gross, looking at the general development of American literature in the characterization of the Negro, feels that the trend has been from stereotype to archetype. For some authors, the pattern has been more complicated because their subject matter may demand a certain type of character. Thus, the contented slave is a natural part of plantation fiction, the arrogant malcontent is equally essential to post-World War I novels, and today the dignified Negro educator satisfies the needs of most integration novels. Nor have the authors found that their best novels are invariably the ones in which they have most conscientiously avoided stereo-typing Negroes. Faulkner's characterization of Negroes in *Requiem for a Nun* and *Intruder in the Dust* may be among his best, but few critics would judge these novels equal to those with the stereotypes or near-stereotypes—*The Unvanquished* and *The Sound and the Fury*. But in these, Faulkner's real virtue is in seeing and portraying a type of Negro while recognizing he can use the white version of the Negro mammy or Sambo without conforming in every detail to the accepted stereotype.

Clearly the Negro experience in the South is different from the white. And just as clearly, there must be some consequently distinctive racial patterns. The temptation to categorize the entire race according to easy and superficial description has proven too strong to resist for many Southern writers. The more sensitive and astute writer may be eager to see resemblances within the members of the group, to perceive a racial type, even though he may consider this the result of conditioning rather than of racial heredity. Here the author walks the tightrope between nice distinctions: On the one side lies derogation of a race to preserve illusive white supremacy, on the other lies the insistence that men are so completely individual that they bear no common racial traits at all. In his effort to avoid the one fallacy, the author may appear to lean too far toward the other. As a consequence, several Southern writers intent on seeing Negroes as atypical of their race incline instead toward seeing them as barely human. Truman Capote's Margaret in *The Grass Harp,* for example, is the eccentric result of rejecting Southern prejudicial stereotyping. She refuses to admit that she is a Negro, claims (against all contrary evidence) that she is an Indian, refuses to replace her missing teeth with dentures, stuffs her mouth with cotton to shore up her collapsing jaws, and thereby also reduces her speech to complete incoherence.

Underlying the derogatory and compensatory stereo-types of the Negro in modern Southern fiction is the overall Southern pattern of thought, a pattern incidentally which is in the process of radical revision. Hamilton Basso had one of his characters express the common white man's attitude of the 'thirties alliteratively, if crudely, by saying, "Niggers do just three things—fight, fornicate, and fry fish."[5] More recently, Ralph Ellison, a Negro writer, also has a character characterize this primitive quality in Negro life. During a riot in Harlem, pictured in *Invisible Man,* two Negro men are talking. One says that the night is "'bout like the rest. . . . 'Cause it's fulla fucking and fighting and drinking and lying—" and finishes his observation with the ironic request, "Gimme the bottle." This "basic savagery" (in Vachel Lindsay's succinct phrase) appealed to the local colorists and admirers of the exotic primitive of the 'twenties and 'thirties more than it does to modern authors.

The assumed inferiority of the Negro has been predi-cated largely, according to Couch, on his physical dif-ferences from the white man rather than on his different life-style: "his color, his crinkled hair, his long skull, prognathous jaw, flat nose, thick everted lips, thin fore-head, long arms, spindly shanks, flat feet, and larkspur heel"[6] —in short the physical characteristics of the Sambo stereotype. Even today, few authors see beauty in the real Negroid features. The more attractive Negro characters almost invariably have Caucasian features. Ellison, Bald-win, and others are concerned with the consequent sense of inferiority bred in Negroes, who resort to skin-bleaches and hair-straighteners. Ellison insists he does not want to be white, and he makes his only really heroic character in *Invisible Man,* Tod Clifton, a pure Negro: "The young man was moving with an easy Negro stride out of the shadow into the light and I saw that he was very black and very handsome, and as he advanced mid-distance into the room, that he possessed the chiseled, black-marble features sometimes found on statues in northern museums and alive in southern towns." Later in *Invisible Man,* Ras (the racist) insists on the Negro-ness of Tod (who was earlier described as an Afro-Anglo-Saxon): "You six foot tall, mahn, You young and intelligent, You black and beautiful—don't let 'em tell you different!" Ras tells Tod that he would be a chief, a black king in Africa, while in America, "You got bahd *hair!* You got thick *lips!* They say you stink!" Here we see the artist recognizing the group characteristics, noting the prejudicial judgments, and trying to see the psychology of the characters involved—a formidable artistic chore. When later in *Invisible Man,* Tod discovers he has been a puppet for the Brotherhood, he combines his discovery of manipulation by whites, stereotyped physical traits, and assumption of the Negro's unfailing good nature in a single symbol. He laughs bitterly at himself and at his gullibility by hawking Sambo dolls on the sidewalk, dolls that are cheap, that are easily controlled in their ludicrous dance by invisible strings, and that have two grinning, caricatured faces.

The tradition of the Negro as a foul-smelling creature, based Couch says "on the fact of a distinct racial odor, and the necessity of doing strenuous, sweaty jobs and living in homes without plumbing—and the general ignorance of white people that they also have a characteristic racial odor which may be offensive to other races,"[7] is used by numerous Negro and white authors. Wright and Ellison both comment on the Negro's awareness of this criticism,

Faulkner uses it regularly in his description of Negro cabins, and Hamilton Basso has one of his characters give up his successful attempt to pass for white partially because he is so tired of fearing that his odor is detectably Negroid.

Such blanket categorizing of Negroes appears in story after story. James Silver attributes this insistence on categorical inferiority to slave-holders' need to justify enslaving the Negro by showing slavery to be his natural state. The Negro was, and often is, "regarded by most whites, and possibly by himself, as being shiftless, apathetic, capricious, untrustworthy, lacking in initiative, unstable, insensitive, and for the most part, an amiable but happy beast perfectly adapted to his wretched position. By and large," continues Silver, "he played the role of Sambo well, giving little visible indication of a conviction that life could be better, or any apparent hope or desire to share in the white man's privileges."[8] Another social critic echoes this Sambo image in his survey of attitudes prevalent in the South until very recently: Most Southerners believed that "Negroes are docile but irresponsible, loyal but lazy, humble but given to lying and stealing—in short, carefree, happy-go-lucky, amoral, dependent children, albeit children with a powerful sexual drive and a lot of rhythm. Until very recently," says Silberman, "this was the image of the Negro almost invariably projected by theater, films, and radio: witness the popularity of Stepin Fetchit and Amos and Andy."[9] This Sambo role recurs in Southern literature, often effectively—i.e., Nigger Jim and Ned McCaslin.

Sterling Brown has said that white authors dealing with the American Negro have consistently interpreted him in such a way as to justify his exploitation. "Creative literature has often been a handmaiden to social policy."[10] So the pictures in earlier literature were often portraits of this "perfect, natural slave." Even the earlier literary critics analyzing the Negro characters in American literature often felt that the caricatures were in truth great works of artistic perception. (One critic is especially entertaining—albeit unwittingly—as he argues how Booth Tarkington portrays realistically and subtly the Negro character in *Penrod*.)

Faulkner, who knew better than to believe in the irrevocable truth of categories, felt that the common racial experience had produced a cluster of typical racial traits. "They will endure," he said of the Negroes. "They are better than we are. Stronger than we are. Their vices are vices aped from white men or that white men and bondage have taught them: improvidence and intemperance and evasion—not laziness: evasion of what white men had set them to, not for their aggrandisement or even comfort but his own." And in addition: "Promiscuity. Violence. Instability and lack of control. Inability to distinguish between mine and thine." And their virtues: endurance, "and pity and tolerance and forbearance and fidelity and love of children. . . . whether their own or not or black or not."[11]

Faulkner's listing is not altogether insulting (although some Negro critics interpret it as patronizing): it is full of perception and of sympathy with the role of the Negro and his need to accommodate his actions to the powerful whites who dominate his life. But it is dangerous to lump a whole people together and expect all the individuals to steal or avoid work or lie or slash one another with razors. Racial typing is perilously close to stereotyping. And even Faulkner sometimes steps over the line.

Ralph Ellison rejects the racial stereotype on the grounds that it allows an author to avoid thought. "The artist," says Ellison, "is no freer than the society in which he lives, and in the United States the writers who stereotype or ignore the Negro and other minorities in the final analysis stereotype and distort their own humanity."[1][2] The stereotype, then, is a refusal to come to grips with the ambiguity, diversity, and complexity of human nature. To classify Negroes, as Ellison feels most Southerners do even today in two categories: "good niggers" and "bad niggers"—the one the suffering servant, the other the hairy ape—is to ignore their humanity and to reject the anguish of recognition that could enrich thought and art. When the artist accepts codified patterns of thought, he is usually embracing facile, shallow fictions and rejecting the density of texture that the more tragic perceptions would allow him. Yet in spite of the demonstrated iniquity of such techniques, most Southern writers do reflect their society by their insistence on racial patterns underlying individual actions or their exaggerated rejection of all patterns.

When authors succumb to the prejudicial or laudatory responses of society and portray a group by reducing its members to the lowest common denominator, ignoring the possibility of individual deviations, they are guilty of stereotyping. What one age may see simply as typing, another age may more clearly understand as stereotyping. The process is seldom conscious, and rarely artistic whether conscious or not. For one thing, it separates one age from another: The prejudices of another age or country are immediately obvious to the alien reader. For another it is often such an absurd parody of human nature that it reflects a shallow and sterile intellect as well as a serious limitation of artistry.

When the stereotype is an incidental portion of the story, it may be compensated for by other virtues—as in

Robinson Crusoe. Here the delight in the adventures and the author's incredible efforts at establishing credibility are more memorable than the inherently contradictory portrait of the noble savage and natural slave, Crusoe's man Friday. Even such a well-intentioned author as Harriet Beecher Stowe may accept the prevailing views of Negro character. But here, the book has its compensations as a document of social history if not as a masterpiece of Negro psychology. The author may use the stereotype as a starting point from which he gradually reveals the individual—as in *Huckleberry Finn*. Or he may use it as a commentary on popular thought and consequent psychological problems, as in *Light in August*. Authors have found myriad subtle possibilities in the use of the stereotype as a tool for their artistry. Consequently, this study is not simply an effort to isolate and condemn stereotyping; it is also an investigation of the materials that good artists and poor ones share and a probing into those perceptions and techniques which raise the Sambo to the Nigger Jim, and the tragic mulatto to the Joe Christmas.

Until recently, very few authors have been able to pierce the veil of idealization or stereotyping to look honestly at the Negro. Noble savages populated eighteenth-century fiction and philosophic mammies replaced them in the nineteenth century. Even Negro writers have been inclined to adopt anti-stereotype stereotypes in their depiction of Negro characters. And such a defender of Negroes as Mrs. Stowe accepts the usual catalogue of Negro stereotypes: the tragic mulatto, the comic Sambo, and the faithful retainer. Such a literary giant as Mark Twain stands virtually alone in nineteenth-century American literature as an artist who saw beneath the familiar mask and the black skin to the human being.

Our own century has witnessed a remarkable revolution in Negro characterization: the Negro has metamorphosized from stereotype to archetype within a few years. Although the change has been apparent in South African writing as well, it has been America that has produced the preponderance of the new Negro-centered literature. And much of the dramatic alteration has been most apparent in the section of America where we least expect change—in the South.

The South has seen more drastic changes in the nature and status of Negroes than has the North and has had more conspicuous reasons for concentrating on this alien but familiar group within its boundaries. Furthermore, the Southern renaissance has provided the talents essential for a significant and aesthetic treatment of Negro characters. Poets, playwrights, and novelists have blossomed forth prodigiously in the South during the last few decades, and the novelists have given especial attention to Negro characters. Some have retained the old stereotypes—both mediocre writers like Margaret Mitchell and more able ones like Stark Young—but a great number have sought honestly to perceive the truth behind the stereotype, to portray humanly the motivations and movements, and to extract universal statements from individual characterizations. Among the Southern literary writers of this group, such people as William Faulkner, William Styron, Carson McCullers, Richard Wright, Ralph Ellison, and Robert Penn Warren are prominent.

While the Northern writer about the Negro has found himself engrossed with problems of the ghetto and of discrimination, the Southerner has been able to explore the individual problems, the human relationships, the needs of the sensitive human being in a static and brutal world. As a result, the Southern novels tend to be character studies, fables of sudden violence, tragedies of isolation, or sagas of attempted escape. They are only occasionally proletarian novels of urban industrial life; rather, they are most often psychological studies set in small towns or on farms. And this isolation appears to be a significant factor in the breaking of the stereotypes. For the Southern writer need not see his characters as social symbols or victims of environment. He need not use them to prove a point, but may rather let their lives and thoughts propose universal themes to the perceptive reader. The better Southern writers tend to be wary of excessive social significance in their novels and stories. Yet their sensitivity to their milieu forces them to try to see things—and people—as they are and to search for significance in human activity and personality.

Those artists who are most nearly free of the tendency to oversimplify Negro characters are the best of the white novelists and the majority of the Negro novelists. Ralph Ellison (who is almost a Southerner—an Oklahoman—and a product of Southern parents and a Southern college) is by far the most subtle and penetrating of the novelists in his presentation of Negro psychology. More prolific, less cerebral, but also powerful in his Negro characterizations, is another Negro Southerner, Richard Wright. (He uses the Southern setting, however, in only part of his fiction since the bulk of his work was produced after he migrated North.)

In Ellison and Wright, and often in Faulkner and Caldwell and Warren and McCullers and other Southern writers, we feel that the Negro character does transcend his Negroness to become not Negro but man.[13] Although by no means an intrinsic or exclusive test for good fiction, the realistic and meaningful characterization of Negroes is certainly interesting to analyze. And in the world of the Southern writer, who has so long been haunted by the shadow of the Negro, it is often a test of his perceptiveness, his imagination, his creativity, and of his humanity.

FAITHFUL AND FAITHLESS RETAINERS

Although the Negro appeared in American literature very early, he usually appeared as the noble-savage-companion type. Mark Twain was one of the few nineteenth-century authors who used the Negro not simply as a personification of Rousseau's idealistic primitivism, or as a symbol of enslaved humanity, or as a caricature of merry menials, but as a real human being. Ralph Ellison is especially fond of Nigger Jim, who reveals himself so fully to Huck and who shows Mark Twain's ability to look behind the platitude. *Puddin'head Wilson* is a less successful, more awkwardly symbolic, and unfortunately didactic effort at exploring the effects of environment on members of different races. For the most part, authors of the deep South have failed to follow Mark Twain's lead until recently. They turned instead to a set of stereotypes which served to shield them from any real understanding of Negro humanity.

Traditionally, the Negro has appeared most frequently in the roles enumerated and elaborated by Sterling Brown: the contented slave, the wretched freeman, the comic Negro, the brute Negro, the tragic mulatto, the local color Negro, and the exotic primitive. Each of these obviously fits into certain formulae: the slave, comic, and freeman are *de rigueur* in plantation novels, those trite old tales of

magnolias, hoop skirts, aristocratic ideals, swashbuckling
young swains fighting for the Southland and for Southern
womanhood, the Negro mammy comforting her white
"chillun"; happy, simple-minded darkies picking cotton,
eating watermelon, and singing spirituals; wicked Yankee
overseers exploiting and abusing ignorant colored folk
without the benevolent owner's knowledge or consent,
causing the foolish darkies to run away from home to the
miseries of freedom, only to return when they have
learned the cruel lessons of poverty and hunger. Hugh
Gloster pictures "the unspeakable charm that lived and
died with the old South" as it is portrayed in the novels of
Thomas Nelson Page, Joel Chandler Harris, Walter Hines
Page and numerous others of the popular post-bellum
writers:

On a broad canvas he paints a stately mansion presided over by
lovely ladies and gallant gentlemen who wear imported finery, enjoy
horse-racing and other gentle diversions, and dispense prodigal
hospitality. The attitude of these cavaliers toward their slaves is
cordial, kindly, benign, and sometimes devoted. The contented
bondsmen appear proudly engaged as servants in the big house or as
laborers in the fields. Near the quarters are prankish picaninnies
romping gleefully in youthful abandon and black veterans resting
comfortably in their declining years. Particularly emphasized is the
loyal relationship between the master and the servant, the mistress
and the maid, the Negro mammy and her charges. The slave received
commendatory treatment for showing courage, fortitude, and
self-sacrifice in relieving the destitution and distress of the Southern
aristocracy during and after the war. In general, however, the Negro
is presented as a simple, contented, comic, credulous, picturesque,
and sometimes philosophical character, gifted in singing, dancing,
tale-telling and reuniting estranged white lovers.[1]

Lest the reader believe that this is the quaint taste of a
bygone age, let him recall that *Gone With the Wind* made
Margaret Mitchell a fortune by reviving this tradition and
immortalizing it in an apparently indestructible techni-

color film. Numerous scenes from other modern novels, for example Frances Gaither's *Follow the Drinking Gourd,* show clear adherence to this old Southern mythology. Certainly not all ante-bellum novels being written today reek of such shallow thought: Robert Penn Warren's *Band of Angels* or Allen Tate's *The Fathers* are hardly idyllic presentations of the role of the slave and the mulatto offspring in the ante-bellum South. But this criticism only reinforces the earlier comment that the better writers eschew the temptation to accept without question received opinion. Faulkner may have been tempted to sentimentalize the Southern aristocracy and the loyal slaves in *The Unvanquished,* but his characters have an individualism and a veracity not typical of the literary plantation tradition.

The contented slave, whose lot it was to till the cotton fields of the old South, conforms to the general outline of the Sambo traits: Physically, he is strong but unattractive and virtually sexless, mentally and morally, he is clearly inferior to whites. Not only the older plantation novelists, but the more recent neo-confederates—Donald Davidson in his poem "The Tall Men," and Allen Tate in his study of *Jefferson Davis, His Rise and Fall*—use some of the underlying concepts of the contented slave tradition. Sterling Brown is clearly incensed at the whole attitude of the Agrarian Reformers, whose manifesto *I'll Take My Stand* includes some of the most reactionary of modern comments on the Southern Negro. But these men are hardly so unthinking or so unfeeling as the old Dixon-Page school, and they do develop their characters from some direct observation as well as abstract theories.

If the Southerner is to write honestly of the South, he is even now obliged to include a type of contented Negro servant or loyal retainer in his stories. Although the real

life character is disappearing, she is still a significant part
of Southern memory. Reminiscences of childhood must
perforce include her portrait, and considering the usual
nature of childhood reminiscences, the portrait will usually
be somewhat sentimentalized.

For example. William Faulkner dedicated *Go Down,
Moses* to "Caroline Barr, Mississippi (1840-1940) who was
born in slavery and who gave to my family a fidelity
without stint or calculation or recompense and to my
childhood an immeasurable devotion and love." Caroline
Barr is one of many actual counterparts of the fictional
mammies so prevalent in Southern literature. Lillian Smith
calls this white-child-colored-nurse affection one of the
three "ghost relationships" that haunt the mind of the
South and give shape to Southern lives and souls. (The
other two ghost relationships, discussed in later chapters,
are white man and colored woman, white father and
colored children.)[2] The Negro mammy—in her roles of
nurse, witchdoctor, priest, intercessor, wet-nurse, comforter, permissive earth-mother—is still so intrinsic a part of
the Southern memory that even the most vicious politicians, appealing to the basest emotions of their Negro-
baiting audience, must yet tip their hats to "the memory
of the humble black mammy of my childhood, to whom I
came for solace and comfort."[3]

Roark Bradford pictures the typical superannuated
mammy in his short story "Cold Death" (included in the
Southern Harvest collection of stories). This old Negro
woman loves and understands all children, black and white
(as Faulkner had his character say is typical of the
Southern Negro). She expresses this love in part by making
quilts for newborn babies, and plans to present her
masterpiece, a Star of Bethlehem quilt, to the baby Jesus
when she sees Him in glory. It is "only manners" to take

Him something, and this is the best that she has to offer. Her trip to the Hereafter is abruptly delayed when she hears the wail of a child who needs a sugar tit and her soothing ministrations. The Angel Gabriel waits impatiently for this obstinate old human to finish with the child so he can carry her off to heaven. The story is typical of Bradford, who condescendingly pictured whimsical Negro religious attitudes. (His *Ole Man Adam and His Chillun* became the basis for the more famous *Green Pastures,* a classic example of superior white laughter at Negro simplicity.) The mammy as a character is lovable and compassionate and perfect for sentimentalizing because she makes no demands on the white memory; there is no need to respect her faith or her rights. Hodding Carter's politician characteristically allies the Negro servant with the contented slave tradition by emphasizing her humility and loyalty—slave virtues so characteristic of the mammy character. She "endures" but makes no effort to "overcome."

Such a character becomes a useful tool in a white-centered novel. Her simple faith, benevolence, comforting words, folk wisdom, and unchanging love make her a refuge for the confused or frightened whites in the story. Elizabeth Spencer, for instance, uses Aunt Mattie in her novel *Voice at the Back Door* to help Tinker feel more secure when her husband has hurt her feelings. Aunt Mattie (the appellation for the character may be *auntie* or *mammy*) has nursed every white child in the community, coaxing them to eat (by putting a little bacon grease on the spoon with the food) when their own mothers could not. And it is to her that the confused white sophisticate turns when confronted with elemental human needs.

Clearly the best use of this figure has been made by William Faulkner, doubtless drawing on his own memories of Caroline Barr for his classic portrait of the mammy in Dilsey and of Molly Beauchamp. Irene C. Edmonds comments that Dilsey has basically the elements of the old Negro mammy stereotype, but that she becomes more than an individualized version of this and more than the stereotype itself in the course of *The Sound and the Fury*: "To him she was a force, a symbol of endurance, a nostalgic reconstruction of remembered past."[4] Dilsey's epitaph in the book is simply "They endured." She therefore is the yardstick by which we measure the strengths, the weaknesses, the frenzies, and the tragedies of the Compsons. She has seen the first and the last; she has watched the fall of the house of Compson and has understood the besetting sins of its members, and she has endured that fall. She has understood Caddy's shame, Jason's cruelty, Quentin's loneliness, and Benjy's idiocy. She has loved and protected the helpless, the incompetent, the childlike members of the family, smoothing over their hurts, but unable to avert their tragic destiny. As Cleanth Brooks comments, "In contrast to Mrs. Compson's vanity and whining self-pity, Dilsey exhibits charity and rugged good sense." "When her daughter Frony warns her that folks will talk if she takes Benjy to church with her, she squelches Frony with, 'Whut folks? . . . And I know whut kind of folks. Trash white folks. Dat's who it is. Thinks he aint good enough fer white church, but nigger church aint good enough for him.' "[5]

Dilsey is clearly and lovingly presented with characteristics that differentiate her from the traditional mammy of inexhaustible humor and gargantuan fleshiness. She is not a "middle-aged Polyanna" nor is she stout. She had once been a big woman, but now the unpadded skin is loosely draped upon the "indominable skeleton" which is left "rising like a ruin or a landmark above the somnolent and impervious guts, and above that the collapsed face that gave the impression of the bones themselves being outside the flesh, lifted into the driving day with an expression at once fatalistic and of a child's astonished disappointment." What the expression means, says Mr. Brooks, "is best interpreted by what she says and does in the novel, but the description clearly points to something other than mindless cheeriness. Dilsey's essential hopefulness has not been obliterated; she is not an embittered woman, but her optimism has been chastened by hurt and disappointment." Although we have no such interior view of her mind as we have of other characters in *The Sound and the Fury*, we still know much of her thought and can identify with her sufficiently to guess even more.

Brooks makes another important point regarding Dilsey when he comments that Faulkner is wise in not attributing her virtues to "some mystique of race in which good primitive folk stand over against corrupt wicked white folk." She herself has no such delusions, is fully aware of her son's inadequacies, for example, and has a fairly conservative Christian faith in original sin: "men are not 'naturally' good but require discipline and grace."[6] She is not a noble savage whose poverty and status as a member of a deprived race assure her of nobility, but is simple enough to be free of the perversions of abstraction and self-obfuscation so typical of Faulkner's whites. Brooks says, "Faulkner's Negro characters show less false pride, less false idealism, and more seasoned discipline in human relationships" than do his whites.[7] For such people, life does have meaning, a Christian purpose abandoned by the more cerebral and agnostic white people.

Faulkner is certainly not alone in using the mammy to point up the comforts and values of a simple Christian faith and to contrast the paganism of modern whites.

William Styron copies this quite blatantly in *Lie Down in Darkness*. The scene in which the white funeral cortege is intercepted by the Negro religious procession clearly juxtaposes the dead values of the whites and the living values of the blacks. The sermon of Daddy Faith delivered to an enthusiastic crowd of Negroes emphasizes their similarities to the Israelites, and underscores the Dilsey virtue of endurance: "We done seen a tough time, my people, all dese years," says Daddy Faith. "We done had de wars and de pestilenches and de exiles. We had de plagues and de bondages and de people in chains. Isr'el has suffered in de land of de pharoach and de land of Nebucherezzar." But the Negroes, despite their sufferings, or because of them, have survived and strengthened their faith, while the whites of the post-war world pictured by Styron have inherited the doom of the benighted South and the fruits of the lost generation to become a tragic, lost people. All of the white people in the story are divorced from their faith, even the minister has lost touch with his fountainhead. They are alienated and sick, and their pattern of corruption contrasts graphically with the fundamental and wholesome quality of faith exhibited by the Negroes. Styron even has the specific mammy character in Ella Swan, who echoes the role of Dilsey, performing the same choric function in the midst of the tragic action.

Even the less complex authors of the 'twenties, DuBose Heyward and Julia Peterkin, frequently employed these same characteristics embodied in the comforting mother figure. A religious Negro matron hovers over Porgy and Bess and tries to save them from their own weaknesses; and a Negro auntie worries over the iniquities and cynicism of Scarlet Sister Mary and tries to reform and help her. These characters, however, are more in the line of good neighbors than are the mammy characters, since the white-black relationship is basic in portrayals of the mammy figure. And their religion is a part of their old-fashioned quaintness—not typical of the young people of either race.

In recent years there have been variations on the mammy role. In some cases, for example, the sympathetic voice of the mammy commentator has been replaced by the sinister black laughter of the knowledgable but uninvolved Negro witnesses to white action. This is in conformity with the thesis that Negroes know the most intimate workings of the white world, while the Southern white has only the most superficial knowledge of Negro life.

Erskine Caldwell, for example, uses Negroes as commentators on the frenetic activities of his sub-human creations. Negroes laugh softly in the background of the Lesters' activities through much of *Tobacco Road*, as Negroes tend to laugh or sneer at white trash through much of Southern literature. In a literature so thoroughly romantic as the Southern, the old role of the voice of reason, the yardstick by which we measure the rationality of the characters, has been replaced by the voice of folk wisdom. The age and sexlessness echo the role of the classic observer, Tiresias. Even in more sophisticated stories, such as Lillian Hellman's *Toys in the Attic*, a Negro serves as commentator on the degeneracy and inhumanity of the whites. Miss Hellman, who used another Negro as her spokesman in *The Little Foxes*, tends to fall into the Faulkner tradition of Negroes representing wisdom of the heart.

The movie version of *Baby Doll*, directed by Elia Kazan, added Negro laughter to Tennessee Williams' story, forming a sinister commentary on the erotic playfulness of the oddly matched pair on a summer afternoon. The dark laughter does have a blood-curdling effect on the audience

and on the characters. In Stribling's *The Store*, Colonel
Vaiden walks through the streets of his home town after
he has stolen the cotton which is to form the basis of his
fortune. With the laughter ringing in his ears, he knows
that the Negroes are aware of his crime. They represent no
actual peril to his fortunes, but they do evoke shame and
embarrassment. Theirs is the Lucretian laughter of impas-
sive viewers, nonparticipants in the white drama.

The laughter may change, in the case of a more
concerned Negro character, to a head-shaking muttering.
Negroes seldom dare speak out so clearly as in Miss
Hellman's plays, but are more likely to follow the pattern
of the old yardman in Flannery O'Connor's "The Displaced Person," who talks and sings to himself outside the
open window, thereby communicating his ideas without
openly inviting the displeasure of Mrs. McIntyre, his boss.
This "accommodation behavior," sociologists explain, is
typical of the Southern Negro, who must express his
displeasure through indirect means.

The whole whimsical, loving, enduring stereotype of the
loyal mammy and her choric descendants is, of course, a
remnant of the plantation tradition in literature. Most
often she is accompanied by the placid and wise Uncle
Toms; the giggly, dim-witted Prissys; the grumbling,
talented, tyrannic cooks. Modern examples of these
ante-bellum types appear in such modern novels as Frances
Gaither's *Follow the Drinking Gourd*, Ovid Williams
Pierce's *The Lonesome Porch*, Allen Tate's *The Fathers*,
and Donald Joseph's *Straw in the South Wind*. They
continue to be popular, appealing as they do to the
memories of the South and to the hopes of the North,
catering to the man who would prefer to think of slaves as
contented and servants as happy. Incidentally, the novels
listed here do not by any means cater so blatantly to this

taste as do many of the more melodramatic and popular-
ized mediocrities. A master must be benevolent indeed to
keep his slaves so contented, and in a large number of
Southern novels we find a tacit or sometimes explicit
preference for paternalism.

William Faulkner saw that the picture of the faithful
slave-servant was often inadequate. Perhaps the mammy
did indeed love the white child as Molly Beauchamp did in
"The Fire and the Hearth" (in *Go Down, Moses*). Still,
how would her husband react to her love of a white child,
and how would the love of the white child alter her
relationship to her own black child? What does the white
father feel about his child's being nursed by a Negro, and
raised in a Negro home? How does the child feel when he
begins to realize that his mammy and his best friends are
"niggers"? What does the mammy feel when her white
child becomes a white man and rejects her hearth and
home? What does the white man feel when he can no
longer eat and sleep with his Negro family as equals, and
who yet feels obliged to return once a month to bring his
mammy a small sack of the soft cheap candy she loves and
a tin of tobacco? Faulkner worried through the labyrin-
thine emotions winding beneath the superficially idyllic
and simple child-mammy relationship.

Robert Penn Warren also has seen the psychological
complexity of the relationship and has chosen to explore
this in his *Brother to Dragons*, a novel in verse. He first
presents his mammy, Aunt Cat, as the classic stereotype:

> . . . She was a good old thing
> And she'd been Lilburn's nigger Mammy, too,
> And gave him tiddy like he was her own
> And loved him good, and loved him still,
>   her Chile.[8]

When her "chile" is in trouble, she refuses to report him,

but her protection of him is Janus-faced, as are all human actions. We do not know whether love of him or hatred of others explains her action, nor can we know how much of the action is an effort to bind him more firmly to her. For we do begin to see that love is a weapon for her:

> She loved him, sure
> But that's not all, for even love's a weapon,
> Or can be a weapon. Let's take the situation,
> Now anybody raised down home—down South—
> Will know in his bones what the situation was.
> For all those years Aunt Cat had fought in silence
> For Lilburn's love, for possession of her Chile,
> With the enemy, the rival, Lucy Lewis.
> The rival had all the armament and power:
> The natural mother, warm and kind and white.
> The rival whose most effective armament
> Is the bland assumption that there is no struggle—
> It is a struggle, dark, ferocious, in the dark,
> For power—for power empty and abstract,
> But still, in the last analysis, the only
> Thing worth the struggle.
>
> This much Aunt Cat knows,
> And knows she has one weapon, only one,
> And the weapon is love. So when the mother's dead,
> Cat's sympathy and love is proclamation and triumph
> Over the fallen adversary . . . .

So her "Chile," seeing her motive, turns against her, hating her and trying to hurt her, saying that he would willingly spit out the milk of that black breast if he could thereby rid himself of what was hers in him. He will not accept her love and refuses to think of her as a surrogate mother.

Here again, then, we have Warren ripping the mask off the stereotype to show us the raw emotions underneath. He enjoys gazing through the placid surface of life to discover the depths of human evil beneath. The struggle for power is not simply between mammy and child or between black and white. It is the recurrent battle of the generations: the fight of the child to free himself from the parent and of the parent to entwine the child with love and guilt and obligation. It is the battle between women to possess men—husbands, sons, and fathers—and that of the men to free themselves from these ensnaring females. For women love often involves a need to possess which is at root not love but will-to-power. But the evil itself is not simple either, enmeshed as it is with blind love. Warren's man is truly an amphibian, and no mammy he presents can long conform to a racial type. She alters rapidly into a symbol of a universal human problem.

William March has a somewhat less Freudian example in *Come in at the Door*. Here the mammy is in addition the mistress to the decadent white aristocrat and mother to a flock of mulatto children. She is a real woman with passions, affections, selfishness, and generosity. With the white boy she has the human and female desire to protect him, to hurt him, and to manage him while justifying herself. Although he learns to despise her, he can not forget her. And even the hatred is not simple or pure.

It is hard for the cynical modern to accept unblinkingly the old picture of the loving mammy, just as hard as it is to believe in unadulterated, selfless love. Now the sentimental old portrait looks servile and somehow repellant. When sycophantic Negroes appear as family servants in Francis Gwaltney's *The Number of Our Days*, we find the author is angry at them for turning against their own people and selling their souls to whites. W.E.B. DuBois set the tone for this attitude in his early study of the faithful servant (in *The Quest of the Silver Fleece*, 1911). "Johnson," says DuBois of his servant character, "was what Colonel Cresswell called a 'faithful nigger.' He was one of those constitutionally timid creatures in whom the servility of his fathers had sunk so deep that it had become second-nature. To him a white man was an archangel, while the Cresswells, his masters, stood for God." DuBois continues this vicious comment on his Uncle Tom character, "He served them with dog-like faith, asking no reward, and for what he gave in reverence to them, he took back in contempt for his fellows—'niggers!' He applied the epithet with more contempt than the Colonel himself could express. To the Negroes he was a 'white folks' nigger,' to be despised and feared."

The "white man's nigger" or the Uncle Tom, or the "handkerchief head" is most frequently now a Bledsoe, a self-seeking obscenity. Lucy Daniels' *Caleb, My Son* is an interesting modern interpretation of a family of "white folks' niggers" who have the reputation for being good, law-abiding, middle-class, loyal Negroes. Suddenly the father discovers that he has a new Negro in his midst, his eldest son, who has left his job with the railroad to become a civil rights agitator. The father first tries to dissuade Caleb, and eventually decides to kill him rather than allow him to ruin the family. Miss Daniels presents the decision sympathetically: Caleb is unattractive and destructive in his ignorant leadership of a group of unemployed hood-lums and his dangerous relationship with a low-class white woman. Therefore the sacrifice of the son is the heroic gesture of a strong man whose pride and whose need for respectability are more valuable to him than his son's life. This is indeed an unusual portrait, picturing as it does with sympathy and irony the middle-class Negro who rejects the whole trend toward action. Here the Uncle Tom is incorporated into the Negro middle-class with its fear of change, its concern for appearances, its betrayal of its own youth.

More often than this Uncle Tom figure, the "white man's nigger" is now the one who acts out the Sambo role. The Sambo, or comic Negro, like Uncle Tom, is a product of the contented slave myth. As Brown explains, any state producing such mirthful types could not possibly be conceived as wretched.[9] Stanley Elkins insists that Sambo really did exist, possibly as a Negro play-act, as a product of race, of slavery, or of our own peculiar variety of slavery. Sambo, whose name became synonymous with "race stereotypes," conformed to the race stereotype cited earlier: "docile but irresponsible, loyal but lazy, humble but chronically given to lying and stealing; his behavior was full of infantile silliness and his talk inflated with childish exaggeration. His relationship with his master was one of utter dependence and childlike attachment: it was indeed this childlike quality that was the very key to his being." As a man, he would have elicited scorn, as a child who stayed in his place, he was both exasperating and lovable. Elkins further comments that Sambo was never considered universal, only *a* plantation type. And the character could be explained as simply a reversion to infantile features of behavior because of his detachment from his background, the shock of the procurement and transport methods used with slaves, or the adjustment to a new, absolute power and to a new environment with little trace of prior cultural sanctions of behavior and personality.[10] Critics mention the parallel to modern concentration camp victims who were often submitted to equally dramatic shocks and frequently exhibited similarly infantile behavior patterns.

This comic Negro type—Sambo or Rastus—whatever his origin in fact later became fixed in the minstrel-show darkey, ludicrous to others and forever laughing at himself. Like Topsy in *Uncle Tom's Cabin*, the comic usually served as the black-faced Elizabethan fool, providing comic relief and folksy wisdom. Roark Bradford drew on this tradition to produce his caricatures of Negro religion; and less talented men such as Octavius Cohen, Arthur Akers, Hugh Wiley, and E.K. Means made him the stock-in-trade of the magazine story. As Brown says of Cohen's work, it was often amusing, but invariably pseudo-Negro—full of improbable situations, condescending attitudes toward Negro professional people, outlandish dialect, malapropisms, and generally propagandistic farce, preaching Negro inferiority and subordination.[11] Obviously this Amos-and-Andy brand of Negro drollery and absurdity is not even relevant to the real folk humor of a character like Uncle Remus or Ned McCaslin, Faulkner's Negro comic in *The Rievers*. The distinguishing marks of the Sambo are his pretentiousness, his love of loud clothes and his "highfalutin" speech, his taste for watermelon and gin, his propensity for chicken stealing, razor fights, and "high yeller" girls. The world that Sambo lives in is as unreal as he is:

The white folks are tolerant, until tenants burn the porches off their homes, or servants mix up affairs too much, when they wax comically profane. The Negroes are superstitious, helpless, cowardly, utterly ridiculous children. Life is easy and indolent except for shrewish wives and scheming crooks; the razors do not cut, the scantlings used by white masters on their menials never hurt, since they strike the head, and the "law" is only a mythical threat. What could be pathos and tragedy sets off laughter.

They all live in a Cloud Cuckoo land that reveals far less of Negro life than of middle-class American taste.[12]

Left-Wing Gordon, hero of Howard Odum's *Rainbow Round My Shoulder*, insists that in spite of (or because of) his gambling, free-loving, happy-go-lucky life, he always gets along well with whites. He is simply satisfying their idea of the Negro, a man without morals or foresight or rancor, a childlike, happy primitive. One modern grinning, womanizing, drinking example is Catfoot Grimes in Hodding Carter's novel *Winds of Fear*. Catfoot is allowed to be the Negroes' source of illegal whiskey in the town because of his humble demeanor and typically Negroid vices. Eventually, when all of his efforts to accommodate to whites prove insufficient to satisfy the lustful and brutal demands of the white-trash sheriff, he is abused and murdered.

It is Ralph Ellison who has offered the classic comments on this character. In *Invisible Man*, an especially obscene Negro has just impregnated both his wife and his eldest daughter; he comments that he has had more attention and money paid him by the whites since he became notorious than ever before. His name, "Trueblood," suggests that he is rewarded because he represents what white men want Negroes to be. The Northern philanthropist, who has sublimated love of his own daughter, senses that Trueblood's incestuous relationship is an acting out of his own libidinous nature. He terms it "chaos," his name for his unspoken and unspeakable desires. During Trueblood's fantastic narrative of his sins, Mr. Norton grows so violently involved that he has either an orgasm or a heart attack—in either case, the vision of chaos proves too much for him. But he mutely acknowledges Trueblood as his alter-ego by giving him a hundred dollars. Ellison seems to think that white men encourage Negro vice not only to prove Negro inferiority but also because the Negroes act out the guilt-ridden lusts of white men and thereby serve a therapeutic purpose.

Thus we see the Southern white indulgently forgiving Negro immorality so long as only other Negroes are involved. So long as Sambo remains, like Jim Trueblood,

servile and dependent, then he can be incestuous, ineffic-
ient, and indolent. He thereby conforms to the role of the
inferior Negro, a childlike creature incapable of shoulder-
ing social or familial obligations, unconcerned for the
future, happy in his "place," content with the day and the
joys thereof.

He is particularly ill-advised to break this pattern,
according to numerous fictional chronicles of the mind of
the South. Erskine Caldwell, T.S. Stribling, and others
show the spontaneous antagonism aroused by an ambitious
or independent Negro. Even as late as the 1940's Victor
Johnson wrote in *The Horncasters* of an ambitious young
Negro war veteran who receives nothing but carping
criticism while the indolent Sambo type is praised for his
obviously inferior work in the fields. When a murder is
committed, although the Sambo has performed the act,
the white community immediately suspects the new Negro
and prepares to lynch him. The Sambo, the classic
innocent, is never really a potentially dangerous character
to the white mind, though Negroes are constantly wary of
him.

The new Southern writers are increasingly suspicious of
the Sambo character. When a man like Robert Penn
Warren portrays a comic Negro in a Sambo costume, he
feels impelled to peel off the grinning mask to reveal the
ironic face beneath it. Even the Sambo name is now
upsetting to most readers—as Faulkner discovered with the
critical reaction against *Intruder in the Dust*. He coolly
allowed his white characters to discuss the Southern race
problem as the problem of "Sambo," and thereby outraged numerous readers so thoroughly that they never
checked to see whether the arguments had any validity or
whether Faulkner himself was indeed laughing at Gavin
Stevens, who was voicing them. We may in time see a

revised Sambo: Ralph Ellison has the requisite sense of humor for devising him, but Ellison has chosen to make his comic Negro a dusky Candide instead. (The grotesque little dancing dolls in the *Invisible Man* are his scathing commentary on the image of Sambo and those who bow to white taste by playing the Sambo-role.) Right now, tensions are too great to allow easy laughter, since most laughter is interpreted as derisive. As a consequence, the modern mood of the race story is usually either tragic or naturalistic or ironic.

To be an Uncle Tom, to the modern, is to lie to yourself or to your world. Ellison has his hero's grandfather define his subservience as *treachery*. The boy is understandably confused: "I was considered an example of desirable conduct—just as my old grandfather had been," says the boy. "And what puzzled me was that the old man had defined it as *treachery*. When I was praised for my conduct I felt a guilt that in some way I was doing something that was really against the wishes of the white folks, that if they had understood they would have desired me to act just the opposite, that I should have been sulky and mean, and that that really would have been what they wanted, even though they were fooled and thought they wanted me to act as I did." So the boy is afraid of the way he acts, and he is afraid to act any other way. He is too honest to lie to himself or to his world, and is therefore viewed by both Negroes and whites as a fool.

The successful Negro, Dr. Bledsoe, is a particularly nauseating example of the "white man's nigger," willing to capitalize on the desires, fears, guilts, and follies of the whites and the Negroes alike to achieve his own ambitions: "Influential with wealthy men all over the country; consulted in matters concerning the race; a leader of his people; the possessor of not one, but *two* Cadillacs, a good salary and a soft good-looking and creamy-complexioned wife." When he goes North, he drops his whining drawl and his obsequious manner, rejecting even his Negro-ness. The invisible man is certain that Bledsoe is a "shameless chitterling eater," but Bledsoe never faces any need to confess or examine his selfish motives. He cynically manipulates those around him, hating the very philanthropists upon whom he fawns while he sings his favorite hymn, "Live a Humble." Here is the Uncle Tom turned into a Babbitt or a Pangloss.

In our day, even Uncle Remus is suspect—witness a 1949 article by Bernard Wolfe, "Uncle Remus and the Malevolent Rabbit." The rabbit is used by Uncle Remus, says Wolfe, to siphon off race hatreds before they possess consciousness. "Folk tales, like so much of folk culture, are part of an elaborate psychic drainage system—they make it possible for Uncle Tom to retain his facade of grinning Tomism and even, to some degree, to believe in it himself."[13]

Certainly, loyal Negro helpers may still appear in literature as they do in life. Calpurnia, the housekeeper-cook of *To Kill a Mockingbird*, is a modernized version of Dilsey. She even takes the lonely children to church with her as Dilsey did Benjy. But Harper Lee portrays her as dignified, educated, and shrewd—not the old servile, self-abasing sycophant of the plantation novel. And Zora Neal Hurston views the Southern pattern of pet Negroes as parallel to the animal-master or at best the child-father one, not a man-to-man friendship between equals (in *Seraph on the Suwanee*). With modern emphasis on motivation and Freudian psychology, there are many new efforts to understand the truth behind the grinning Negro mask of servility and love. And with the growing scarcity of Negro cooks, housekeepers, and mammies who have previously been readily available as cheap labor for any middle-class Southern family, the faithful retainer is becoming rarer in literature.

3

BLACK ULYSSES

Other black and white characters tend to cluster about the faithful mammy: There is usually the noble white aristocrat, whose paternalistic care of an "inferior people unfitted by intellect to be free"[1] is clearly an act of Christian charity justifying slavery and loyal servitude. Otherwise, as Ellison points out, the very contentment is despicable for it becomes a judgment on the people who have sold their souls and bodies for marginal security—a sorry mess of pottage at best. Since the only real tie must be to him, the master, the aristocrat replaces family ties. Therefore, though most novelists show that it is with great personal pain that the owner of slaves in the old plantation novels should do so, benevolent masters do at times separate husbands and wives and children. Echoing Elkins' comment on the Sambo character, Silberman says, "It would be hard to conceive a system better designed to create the submissive, infantile, incontinent, undisciplined, dull, dependent 'Sambo' of Southern legend."[2] Other than the creation of the mammy, the Uncle Tom, and the Sambo, the system also produced the black Ulysses. By destroying family ties, parental responsibility, stable male-female relationship, and cementing only ties to the white aristocrat, the system has emasculated the Negro male.

The faithful mammy is usually paired with the rambling black Ulysses, the ne'er do well male character, without any significant or enduring role in family life, who becomes the wanderer or the Sportin' Life. The mammy's very competence and her role as the family wage-earner (as well as her frequent role as mistress to the white master) allowed and often provoked the man of the house to be both incompetent and irresponsible. Most novels about Negro life point to the absence or delinquency of the father and to the matriarchal family structure centered around the aggressive female. Often, in fact, a dominating grandmother becomes the provider and disciplinarian while the mother follows the careless pattern of her errant husband or lover.

Regarding the historical conditions that these fictional patterns reflect, Eric Lincoln has said, "When Negroes were slaves, neither the law nor the slave owners recognized marriage between slaves. Males of prime physical condition were mated with females, like so many cattle. Children were left with the mother, giving the Negro mother an early, exclusive interest in the family and forcing upon her full responsibility for its care." Styron pictures the broken homes and the lonely fathers as a part of the reason for the slave rebellion led by Nat Turner. One of the key rebels has been separated from his wife and young child and has never recovered. His Sambo-act fools the whites, but Nat knows of the pain behind it and the humiliation and fury in his heart. Even when the "male and female were permitted to live together longer than necessary for procreation," comments Lincoln, "the Negro father (he could hardly be called a husband) had absolutely no control over his family or its fortunes. Children were seized and sold. Often the father himself was sold away from his family, never to see them again." While this process of demoralization and castration was debilitating the Negro man, the Negro woman was gaining social and economic advantages. Her position in the house as mammy, confidante, mistress, cook, and maid gave her opportunities for advancement unavailable to the Negro man. In the post-war South, in which Negro women were frequently paid more than their menfolk, while their men walked the streets looking for work the women could ordinarily find jobs in domestic service.[3]

It is ironical, considering the sentimentality surrounding the fictional Negro mammy, how unattractive the Negro wife and mother can often be. Ellison attributes the unattractive and unfeminine nature of the Negro mother to the paradoxical role she must play. While she can afford to be (and profits by being) loving, generous, and gentle with her white children (a Santa Claus symbol or great warm Earth-Mother), with her own she must serve as bread-winner, teacher, and disciplinarian. To insulate them from the life she knows to be ahead and to prepare them for its cruelty, she must lecture, deprive, and beat her own children. The violent beating scene is a standard climax in the stories of Eden-innocence for the Negro child, building up to the moment he becomes aware of evil—usually when he has been too bold with white children or adults. Then comes the brutal punishment the mother administers out of fear that the child will cultivate a rebellious nature and a tragic career. Ellison comments on Richard Wright's use of this scene in his autobiographical *Black Boy*: "One of the Southern Negro family's methods of protecting a child is the severe beating—a homeopathic dose of violence generated by black and white relationships. Such beatings as Wright's were administered for the child's own good; a good which the child resisted, thus giving family relationships an undercurrent of fear and hostility . . . because the beating is administered by the mother, leaving the child no parental sanctuary. He must ever embrace violence along with maternal tenderness, or else reject, in his helpless way, the mother."[4]

In stories such as Peter Feibleman's *Place Without Twilight*, a remarkable tale of a mother's solicitude for her children, the mother becomes so obsessed with fear for her children that she can find comfort only in their death or in madness. Here, her pathological concern makes the beating so brutal as to alienate or derange the child. In most of the stories, as in Richard Wright's case, the child is so angry that he turns against his mother, but he does remember the lesson. Wright has pointed out the absence of real affection in Negro family life; Feibleman's book would lead us to wonder whether there is time or room for affection when parents are so haunted with fear and so concerned with survival. As John Williams says in his story of such a hard-working Negro mother (in the North this time), *Sissie*, "giving love to children was a luxury she couldn't afford and when she could, she had got out of the habit."

The scene is usually artistically effective. It acts as an initiation rite for the Negro boy, paralleling the senseless brutality he is to anticipate as his life pattern. Ellison pictures life for the Southern Negro male in his ritualistic battle-royal scene at the beginning of *Invisible Man*. The young Negro has escaped the therapeutic violence administered by the usual Negro mother, and must therefore go naively to worse pain because he is ignorant of his actual limitations and potentials. He expects to be rewarded for his work, but is instead sadistically tempted by a white woman, forced to fight other Negroes (instead of his real enemy, the white club-members), scramble on an electrified rug for money he has rightfully earned, and speak humbly in the face of derisive and threatening laughter. Every gesture of the episode is designed to reduce his manhood, his racial pride, his sense of accomplishment.

When the novel centers around the Negro family, the author generally portrays the matriarch as enormously hard-working, inside and outside of the home. She cooks, cleans, washes, and irons with a vengeance, growing increasingly irritated with her lusty husband and their abysmal poverty. She projects herself entirely into her children's lives, causing the father to become the irrelevant member of the household, providing her with more encumbrances, but no help. This is particularly typical of the local-color stories of Julia Peterkin and Paul Green.

In *Rainbow Round My Shoulder*, Howard Odum explores the role of the Negro woman—head of her family, servant of white people, breadwinner, disciplinarian of her children, mistress and victim of her husband. He sees her as one of the most interesting Negro characters available for fiction.

Again, the Negro woman and mother, chiefest of paradoxes in the white and Negro world. Faithful worker and stolid servant. Provider for large families. Revered "Auntie" and "Mammy" enshrined in memory and literature. Faithful, dependable, powerful in prepotency. The woman God forgot. Winner of long distance endurance tests. Yet again "Nigger woman," the lowest standard of personality to certain members of the white race. Considered as of old by white men and white women as not a person but a Negro. Storm center of race mixture. Battleground of Negro men, chief character in Negro song life.[5]

In this syndrome of faithful mammy, faithless wife, sole-provider, authority symbol for the children, and angry mate for the lusty husband, we have the genesis of the black Ulysses, the run-away father in search of adventure and manhood. "The result, all too frequently," says Charles Silberman in regard to this matriarchal pattern, "is more than just psychic withdrawal. Unable to play the usual male role, the husband all too often tries to demonstrate his potency through a display of sexual prowess. But the effort fails as it must, and so he begins to wander and ultimately leaves for good." This desertion, in the meanwhile, helps confirm "what the wife had suspected all along—that men are just no good; her father had deserted *her* mother, and so she has learned in childhood to distrust men—a fact that had interfered with her ability to help her own husband."[6] Thus, the Negro male is continually stripped of his masculinity and is condemned to "a eunuchlike" existence in a culture which venerates masculine primacy.

Most novelists present the wife of the Negro man as submissive and loving only in the early days of the marriage. Julia Peterkin's Scarlet Sister Mary is a good example of the stages of decadence in a typical Negro marriage: her initial eagerness to be a good wife, her husband's gradual loss of interest, her increasing concern for her children, her disillusionment with her husband, and finally her complete rejection of him and fixation of affections on the children. She, in turn, will reflect her hatred of men in the way she brings up her own children: "the sons can fend for themselves but her daughters must be prepared so that they will not have to go through what she has gone through. (Considerably more Negro girls than boys go to college, for example; among whites, the reverse is true.) And so the matriarchy perpetuates itself."[7] Thus the good mother becomes the bad wife of the delinquent husband, or the black Ulysses.

Odum used this black Ulysses or the Negro "bad man"—Railroad Bill or John Henry—as his rambling folk hero, Left-Wing Gordon. This epic figure indulges his "ramblin' mind," using work only as a "marginal survival tool," becoming a useless, charming, happy, lonely, rootless wanderer. His three drives are sleeping, eating, and "joreeing"; his pleasures are drinking, gambling, and womanizing. He dresses well when he can, but does not worry when he can not. Odum insists that he is a "folk soul in the making"—"Black Ulysses, a brown black man, mixed up in a white man's civilization, wandering in a black man's world. Though he travel the whole world over, to the white man he is a Negro or a number. A part of all he had met, yet apart from it. Builder of roads and cities, dependent upon the white man, the white man dependent upon him."[8] To Odum, he is emblematic of the American Negro in the first quarter of the twentieth century and a perfect candidate for heroic adventure tales. Actually he is a character, like the Negro mother, who has great potential artistic value. He conforms to the American Rip Van Winkle, run-away father type (cf. Leslie Fiedler's theories) not to mention the more archetypal Ulysses—the rootless wanderer who waxes sentimental about "Ithaca," but knows he has no real role to play among these dreary people with the tired old wife and the drearily dutiful son. The embodiment of the timeless lust for adventure, he has the makings of a mythic black hero. But the artists have neglected him for the most part and turned instead to the Negro woman he left behind, to the hard-working Negro sharecropper who refuses to follow his pattern, or to the Negro middle-class money-grubber.

One of the few successful efforts to trace the man, rather than stay and sympathize with his abandoned wife, is Millen's *Sweet Man*, the tale of a handsome young Negro driven from his land and his home by the brutal sharecropping system, becoming eventually a kept man, first with Negro women whom he stirs to Frankie-and-Johnny type quarrels in barrooms, and later with white women. Always hoping to return home, he invariably moves further away from a stable existence. Curiously, with all of the conscious and unconscious efforts to castrate the Negro male, authors continue to picture him of super-human, or sub-human, sexual potency.

Although the black Ulysses type is not identical with the brute-Negro stereotype of Reconstruction fiction, he does have some of his characteristics: He is insolent to whites, shiftless, irresponsible, and "animalistic." The first qualities signify that he has proved unwilling to display the fawning loyalty required of good servants, that he was too proud or too wild to become a lap dog or a trained seal. Nat Turner's father left home and family because he was slapped by a white master. No neat butler's uniform could recompense him for this public humiliation. His independence does not involve the need to spread a gospel of freedom or lead a rebellion. Black Ulysses is a disillusioned, cynical, carefree loner, rootless and amoral.

Yet he does bear a certain resemblance to the brute Negro and the wretched freeman of earlier fiction. To certain authors afflicted with clear cases of negrophobia, the brute Negro was a real threat to the unreconstructed South. *The Clansman: An Historical Romance of the Ku Klux Klan* (1905) (the novel by Thomas Dixon later made into the movie *The Birth of a Nation*) offers a classic example of the Negro villain. Again in *The Leopard's Spots*, Dixon elected to spend his limited talent and immense hate on vilification of Yankees and Negroes. The most famous of his scenes is the chase, in which the ape-like Negro pursues the lily-white virgin to her death as she leaps over the cliff to escape a fate-worse-than-death. Here is the Negro hairy-ape as described by Dixon:

He had the short, heavy-set neck of the lower order of animals. His skin was coal black, his lips so thick that they curled both ways up and down with crooked blood-marks across them. His nose was flat and its enormous nostrils seemed in perpetual dilation. The sinister beady eyes, with brown splotches in their whites, were set wide apart and gleamed ape-like under his scant brows. His enormous cheekbones and jaws seemed to protrude beyond the ears and almost to hide them.

The brutality of the Negro seems to be a nineteenth-century euphemism for sexuality. The scene is clearly an intended rape, and the Negro is presented as a repulsive physical mirror to his beastly sexual drives. The legend of Negro lustiness and the hysterical concern for the virginity of white maidens color the scene and exaggerate the brutishness of the Negro male.

An interesting variation of this brute-Negro stereotype appears in Richard Wright's *Native Son*. Here Wright has a parallel near-rape scene, but the irony lies in the corruption of the white woman and the comparative innocence of the Negro man, who kills her out of panic rather than from anger or lust, and who acts out the paradigm of brutishness by chopping up and burning her body—but out of fear, not out of innate brutality or thirst for blood. Hugh Gloster feels that Wright is deliberately selecting the "bad nigger" stereotype to point out that "the individual delinquency is produced by a distorting environment rather than by innate criminality." Wright wanted to use masculine Negro characters, not what Leslie Fiedler calls Clarissa-in-pantaloons—the Uncle Tom. Clearly the faithful retainers are sexless, faithful eunuchs to be trusted with innocent virgins. Styron shows Nat Turner's discomfort at the flirtatious conversation of a young white girl who can not picture a faithful "darky" as having any sexual urges. Thus, in order to bring manly heroes into Negro-centered fiction, Wright needed to blast both Uncle Tom (by Bigger Thomas) and the Negro ape-man (by mitigating his crime and modifying his lust).

Ralph Ellison carries the Negro-rape-of-the-white-virgin

scene even further by having a thoroughly depraved white woman ask her Negro bed-companion to pretend he is raping her. In this grotesquely funny scene, the brute Negro is transformed into a Joseph Andrews as his sexual appetite crumbles before the onslaught of the nymphomaniac Sybil. The enormous change from *The Clansman* to the *Invisible Man* explains the disappearance of the brute Negro. Once we analyze his motives and his background, we have taken the stark brutality away from him and destroyed the stereotype. He was destined to disappear with the Victorian hysteria about sex that he embodied; a post-Freudian world views him as wish-fulfillment rather than as actual peril.

This brute Negro had been insignificant in ante-bellum Southern literature, according to Sterling Brown, because the emphasis was on the removal from savagery to Christianity. Only when insurrection and a desire for freedom loomed on the horizon did Negroes appear in literature as animals fresh from the forest. This animalistic or brute or sexual quality of the Negro, so frequently touted in both literature and society, has led in turn to the classic Southern "cure"—castration.

In most of the stories, the castration is strictly psychological, as is apparent in the role of the Negro man in Southern life and fiction, but it becomes quite literal in the lynch narratives. As will be apparent in the discussion of the black Christ, the usual excuse for the fictional lynch scene is the Negro man's raping of a white woman. This myth of the Negro male's sexual appetite so permeates Southern thought that when a small Negro boy suddenly appears in a white woman's bedroom she is reduced to hysteria (in Frances Gaither's novel *The Red Cock Crows*). For Bigger Thomas (in *Native Son*), the danger of being caught in a white woman's bedroom looms so large as to cause him to panic into the horrible alternative of murder. Wright tells of a friend who was shot by white men because of the suspicion that he was "fooling" with a white prostitute in the local hotel. "I had heard whispered tales," admits Wright in *Black Boy*, "of black boys having sex relations with white prostitutes in the hotels in town, but I had never paid any close attention to them: then those tales came home to me in the form of the death of a man I knew." Wright uses a parallel situation in his novel *The Long Dream*. In this case, the young man is so afraid the police will find a picture of a white girl on him that he wads up the paper and eats it.

When a Negro is castrated for his alleged rape of a white woman in *Sweet Bird of Youth*, Tennessee Williams has his spokesman attribute the gory practice to sex envy. This Freudian explanation for the urge to castrate Negroes has grown increasingly popular in modern fiction. James Baldwin explains away most racial antagonism on this colorful but dubious basis. Although the literary enthusiasm for Negro sexuality may prove only a passing fad, it has been a characteristic distinguishing the Ulysses from his sexless brother on the plantation, Sambo.

4

BLACK SIRENS

In the sub-human portrayals of the Negro brute, authors have in fact emphasized the sexual prowess of females as well as males, although it is the male in particular who is presented as maniacal in his sex urge and super-human in his genital adequacy. Where it is not violent, the Negro's sex urge is characteristically seen as nonetheless uncontrolled as to both its object and the morality of its expression. Although novelists usually present educated Negroes as somewhat more responsible in their sex life, white codes of middle-class morality only partially influence their sexual behavior. For example, Emma, the educated and beautiful wife of the undertaker in Jessie Hill Ford's recent novel, *The Liberation of Lord Byron Jones*, has experimented freely before and after marriage in search of sexual fufillment, which eventually she apparently finds with a Black Muslim leader. In Emma's case, her husband's refusal to relax and enjoy natural pleasure in sex, because he considers sexual abandon a low, "nigger" trait, has complicated her own responses. (In fact, she is not so much a Negro character as a refugee from the Lost Generation tied to a Victorian mate.) In another case (Julia Peterkin's *Black April*) the educated daughter of a plantation cook is only briefly hesitant about committing fornication and later adultery with an attractive but uneducated and irresponsible young man on the plantation.

On a somewhat lower educational level, Negro women are frequently presented as willing partners, though not especially lustful: the neighbor girl in *Place Without Twilight* has slept around so regularly that she has no idea who has fathered her unborn child; she only hopes it was the nice man who bought her the fish sandwich. Nancy Manigoe, the ex-prostitute in *Requiem for a Nun*, has a somewhat more grotesque image for the same thing. She had just had a miscarriage because a man kicked her in the stomach. When Temple asks her whether that man was the father as well as the murderer of the unborn child, Nancy says she does not know: "If you backed your behind into a buzz-saw, could you tell which tooth hit you first?" When Thomas Wolfe's young paper-boy hero tries to collect money from a Negro prostitute, she offers to pay him off in "jelly-roll." But again, this seems less because she is a Negro than because she is a prostitute. George Henderson's Ollie Miss is one of the best examples of a simple, lusty, natural Negro girl, but that style is less typical of modern novelists who are suspicious of exotic folk traits. Stories of Negro women trying to defend themselves against white seducers and rapists are growing increasingly prominent. *Southwind, The Back Door, High John the Conqueror, The Liberation of Lord Byron Jones,* and many others include such scenes.

Although the black siren, like black Ulysses, is often presented as sexually amoral, sprinkling the world liberally with "yard children" or "woods colts," she is seldom pictured as irresponsible. She is concerned for her children, and in her role as protector and provider, often grows to despise the father and to resent his irresponsible sexual indulgence. (In several of the stories, she provides for the child by handing him or her over to a more reliable grandparent and continues on her own path of sexual abandon: *Mamba's Daughters*, and *Southbound* are examples of this pattern.) Paul Green's "The Iron" points up the wife-mother's dilemma. The woman, angry with her husband for his romantic free-lancing and at herself for allowing him to come home periodically to beat, rob, and seduce her, rebels and strikes out at him. The mother of Odum's hero in *Rainbow Round My Shoulder* does the same thing. Tired of indulging the vices and follies of an attractive black Ulysses in her life, she kills him and is readily excused by a white court. These Penelopes grow weary of the spinning and waiting role and bolt for the door against their delinquent Ulysses.

More detrimental to the Negro man's self-respect than his loss of dominance in the household has been his loss of control over his women. The sexual availability of Negro women and the Negro man's inability to wreak revenge on her white seducer/rapist have done much toward the emasculation of the Negro man. He has historically had no power to object to a white man's seducing or raping his wife or mistress—in fact John Dollard points out that it does not even occur to most white Southerners that the Negro man might be as sensitive about the rape of his women as the white man is about the rape of his.[1] He is, in fact, often brutal in his attitude toward Negro women: the myth, often quoted in novels is that no Negro women can be raped because they are always willing (cf., Erskine Caldwell's *In Search of Bisco*).

Ironically, the white woman has never had so much to fear from black men as have black women from white men. Used freely in slavery days, they have been considered fair game by certain classes of whites ever since. The Negro prostitute, predictably, caters to white as well as black men. Witness Nancy Manigoe, for example, and Miss Reba's Negro whore-cook with her gold tooth. Faulkner symbolizes the essential nastiness and insensitivity of a Snopes-type character by having Clarence Snopes go to a Negro whorehouse because it is cheaper than the white one. T.S. Stribling's characters seldom bother looking for black prostitutes; they simply assume that all Negro women are available for their sexual use. When Miltiades loses his fiancee to a rival on their wedding day, he goes right home and rapes the first Negro woman he meets. In a later novel in the same trilogy, *The Store*, Jerry leaves the embraces of his sweetheart so aroused that he seduces the first Negro girl he comes across. And in both cases, the "heroes" have few compunctions and almost no recollection of the incidents.

Negro servants in white homes are especially vulnerable. Ellen Glasgow shows one of her more ruthless characters who has used his Negro washwoman regularly for his sexual gratification, has had a child by her, and has no interest in supporting her or the child, or even in saving the boy's life—in fact, he cannot even recall the boy's name. One of the more detailed and humanized examples of the master-servant sexual union is in Lonnie Coleman's *Clara*. Here the cook and the master of the house have become mutually attracted and have an affair that results in a child—again because of his frustration with white women, and in particular his frigid wife. He is not a brute like Ellen Glasgow's Cyrus, and does indeed love Clara and does provide for their child—to the immense disgust of his childless wife. More often, though, the story is one of pure lust. David Westheimer's *Summer on the Water* shows the flirtation, seduction, and pregnancy that erupt from the need to dominate and possess, not to love. William March's *Come in at the Door* has a similar thesis.

Usually, the nasty old man involved is either decayed gentry (the doctor in Ellen Glasgow's *Barren Ground*, the "alcoholic" aristocrat in Harper Lee's *To Kill a Mockingbird*, or the grandfather in Warren's *World Enough and Time*); or he may be a ruthless red-neck (deputy sheriff in Spencer's *Voice at the Back Door*, Aycock in Gordon's *Reprisal*). The relationship is generally presented as the degenerate pattern of social misfits or sexual bullies. A particularly horrible scene in Jessie Hill Ford's *The Liberation of Lord Byron Jones*, for example, has a policeman raping the wife of a Negro suspect in the back seat of a police car while his partner waits and watches but declines to participate. Her husband performs the classic role of the Negro male reacting to the violation of his wife: He cannot retaliate against the brutal white policeman, he has no recourse in law, he has no white friends who can or will take his part, so he must hurt a Negro in order to release his aggressions: He lashes out at his baby son, beats and kills him—to his enormous grief and horror. It is a perfect symbol of the castrating situation in which he finds himself enmeshed.

Only a few of the Negro male characters dare assert their manhood in the face of aggressive whites. In Ford's novel, the Negro undertaker, Jones, finds that his wife is having an affair with a white policeman. Jones believes that a man—any man regardless of race—has the right to divorce a slut. Knowing that to name a white policeman as adulterer in a divorce action is risking one's life, Jones persists. White lawyers try to discourage him, as does everyone else, but Jones believes that his "liberation" is tied up with his sexual and marital integrity. He dies because he is a "nigger" acting like a white man, but to accept his "niggerness" would have limited his alternatives to death or castration.

Faulkner also rejects the usual focus on the stereotype of the black siren to explore the reactions of her emasculated black mate. Lucas Beauchamp, like Lord Byron Jones, sees the test of his manhood in insisting that his wife be sexually inviolate. When Lucas suspects Zack Edmonds of having relations with Molly, he insists that Molly leave the Edmonds' home, where she is nursing the orphaned white infant, and return home. Lucas makes his suspicions clear to Zack without resorting to an explicit accusation. Zack, who is apparently innocent of any desire for Molly, is outraged, but Lucas wins. The scene is presented as the moment of truth for the Negro man, the moment he affirms his masculinity if not his humanity. In Lucas' case, the gesture is a success, but then it is subtle, it is based on a false suspicion, and he happens to be dealing with a gentleman and a friend. *Southwind* and *Strange Fruit* are more typical stories, showing the Negro husband's and brother's fury, and their decisions to risk murdering the white seducers. Here melodrama replaces Faulkner's more subtle psychologizing.

The fact of the Negro woman's sexual vulnerability is so unquestioningly acknowledged in Southern literature that those times when she escapes abuse become more memorable than the more run-of-the-mill rape scenes. As Aunt Mattie says of her nine-year-old Negro daughter when an old white man catches the child and rapes her, "Nex' time she know to run *'fo'* he sees her, stid of after." (The scene is in Elizabeth Spencer's *Voice at the Back Door*.)

Negro mistresses are prevalent in Southern literature too, as an acknowledgement that relationships between white man and Negro woman are often more permanent than these casual connections would suggest, and may even involve some real affection—not simply lust. Most often the authors agree with Faulkner in seeing this abuse of sex

and of humanity as the curse of the South, more horrible
than the slavery that bred it. Faulkner's "Delta Autumn"
pictures the modern Southerner still unwilling to accept
his Negro mistress as a human being, just as his ancestors in
"The Bear" had abused their slaves sexually. In *Voice at
the Back Door*, the Sheriff's Negro mistress cannot come
to his death bed or his funeral, in spite of their long affair
and real love. Her only consolation is the knowledge that,
for the last fifteen years, Travis loved her better than he
loved his wife. The same helplessness and classlessness of
the Negro mistress are underlined by dramatic scenes in
several Southern novels. For instance, in *Straw in the
South Wind*, the mulatto mistress finds that all of the years
of love and sacrifice and social ostracism can be quickly
forgotten by a middle-aged white man when he encounters
a flirtatious young white girl. The Negro mistresses have
none of the legal rights or the moral backing of the black
or the white community that can be so comforting to
women at times of personal tragedy. The black mistress is
outside the pale. But she does, in this story, have the cold
comfort that her erstwhile lover is so devastated at leaving
her and being rejected by his white sweetheart the same
evening that he commits suicide.

Donald Joseph, the author of this melodrama, uses the
black-white affair to increase the emotions in a less vital
way than Elizabeth Spencer did in *Voice at the Back Door*.
Miss Spencer, although her illicit affair is not central to the
story, is more interested in understanding the people than
in presenting a social message reinforced by violent poetic
justice. She has the ability to draw delicately and
sensitively honest portraits without insisting on a manipulation of her story. There is no reward for the Negro
mistress, other than the quiet memory of a rich relationship. She does not need to see her lover acknowledge her

before the world or disown his legal white wife. Miss Spencer sees that whatever contentment the Negro mistress can have must come from a private knowledge of love and not from social acceptance.

One rare story of the Southern white man and his Negro mistress, Shirley Ann Grau's *Keepers of the House*, follows Miss Spencer's pattern of deep affection by showing the man trying to shore up his mistress against the storms of life. Wanting their children to be legitimate, yet not willing to subject her to the pressures of Southern society, he marries her in secret, out of state. And, hoping to keep his children's racial background from being recorded on their birth certificates, he sends his wife North for childbirth. He thereby escapes the brand of race on them and provides their opportunity to pass for white. Although he has quietly and carefully provided for his wife's welfare in the event of his death, he bows to social convention by doing this without mentioning her in his will. In other words, the white man who loves his Negro woman and his mulatto children must be circumspect in expressing that love.

Miss Grau builds a number of beautiful and subtle scenes from this understanding of and compromise with society. The father never tells his white daughter by an earlier marriage what he is doing, but he does insist on her knowing he acknowledges his paternity of the mulatto children. And when these children are ill, he shows his love as well as his good sense by tricking the doctor into coming, pretending that the white girl, not the mulatto, is ill. Miss Grau uses such scenes effectively for suspense, revelation of character, delineation of the conflict between the nonconformist and his society, and for plot development. Unlike many authors using this theme of miscegenation, she does not appear primarily concerned with sensationalism or social reform.

Harper Lee also avoids the obvious pitfalls of the tale of miscegenation in her brief handling of the old man who feels a similar affection for his mistress and their children. He pretends he is a drunkard so the community will leave him alone and will have a satisfying explanation for his aberration. Sacrifice of reputation seems a small price to pay for personal happiness.

The temptation to love, not simply lust, has grown to be an increasingly popular subject for literature. Paul Green used it in an early play, "White Dresses" (in the *Lonesome Road* collection), and Stribling saw the possibility with his Gracie, who was the beloved mistress of an officer in the Union Army (in *The Forge*) and later of a local store-keeper (in *The Store*). But both of these authors were more liberal than most of the writers of their day. More recent stories of miscegenation, such as *Clara, Summer on the Water,* and *Strange Fruit,* emphasize the affection and intellectual or emotional response between white man and Negro women. The fear of society, the tainted responses to one another, the distrusts inbred by upbringing, the sense of violated taboos—these make such stories interesting psychological and sociological commentaries.

Curiously, the violation of the black-white taboo often results in the violation of the less obvious black-mulatto barrier. Paul Green's mulatto temptress (in "White Dresses"), for example, is forced to marry a Negro whom she finds physically repulsive; color snobbery is found both between and within races. David Westheimer (in *Summer on the Water*) uses the pressures imposed upon his mulatto heroine to accept such a marriage as the motive for her suicide. The girl, a cook in a private home, finds she is falling in love with a young man in her employer's family. When he comes to her one night in her room, driven by affection for her as well as by sexual need, she is delighted. Eagerly accepting his presence, she suddenly discovers he is unconsciously responding to her "nigger-ness" by refusing to kiss her. As he attempts to seduce her without any preliminary displays of affection, she repels his advances. And then, full of anger and need for self-abasement, she races to the bed of a black buck whom she finds physically repellant. Later, when the family tries to force her to marry this black Negro, she strips off her clothes and drowns herself (a symbolic effort to be cleansed of her filth). Westheimer's story is more self-conscious and contrived than Green's earlier, simpler tale, but far superior to that best-selling melodrama, *Strange Fruit*. Warren's *Band of Angels* has a parallel embracing of the black lover when spurned by the white.

Lillian Smith also explores the pressures of society and environment on the individual in a miscegenous affair. Her white lover in *Strange Fruit*, a cad by anybody's definition, must rape his black mistress to prove to her and to himself her "nigger-ness." Miss Smith shows her fantastically long-suffering Negro girl (attractive, educated, decent, and hardworking) full of love for her wretched white seducer and eager to bear his child without concern for her own reputation. Regardless of her selfless devotion and hound-dog loyalty, the villainous white lover must beat and rape her to act out the perverse Freudian psychology that cannot allow him to need and to love her. And she in turn proves a drab little masochist by refusing to despise him as he so richly deserves. Both characters are unbelievable representatives of carefully documented Southern types. Here is a classic example of Aristotle's "possibility" and "probability" thesis—they are real but unbelievable.

As if sexual competition between men and women were not complex enough, when the will-to-power, the need to degrade the opposite member, and the response to the broken taboo also enter in, the result can be emotional and physical chaos. What this whole extra-social pattern of interracial sexual activity does to the white men's wives is still another story. In *Killers of the Dream* (her forthright summary of ideas underlying *Strange Fruit*), Lillian Smith describes the "temptation and menace" of the black temptress in the back yard, the seesaw of "attraction, fear, repulsion, attraction" experienced by the white man, and the response of the white wife. "The race-sex-sin spiral had begun," says Miss Smith. "The more trails the white man made to the back-yard cabins, the higher he raised his white wife on her pedestal when he returned to the big house. The higher the pedestal, the less he enjoyed her whom he had put there, for statues after all are only nice things to look at." The net result of this situation was more numerous "little trails of escape from the statuary and more and more intricately they began to weave in and out of southern life. Guilt, shame, fear, lust spiralled each other. Then suspicion of white women began to pull the spiral higher and higher."[2]

While Miss Smith has been unable to give her analysis valid fictional expression, Edward Kimbrough has given it vitality by dramatizing rather than discussing it. In *Night Fire*, he tells of a Southerner who brings his white bride home and abandons her on their wedding night to go to the bed of his Negro mistress. Later, the childless, frustrated wife grows increasingly angry, venting her hatred on the Negro woman and her tan child. Eventually her fury ends in madness. Samantha, the wife, universalizes her pain and wrath by crying that her story is the story of Southern womanhood: "We are the ones they outraged," she is quoted as saying. "They with their imaginings about the lust of the black they'd enslaved and now feared.

Feared because they'd enslaved him and feared because they were pampered and weak and they could see his strength. And so they named him Lust, and said it would be dangerous to unslave him. That was their first lie, and then they made another one, to make the first one stronger."

This is the lie that really enrages Samantha: The men put their own women on a pedestal to show "how different white was from black. They made the lie that their women had no bodies. And they worked so hard at it, they made us not women at all, but sort of wineless casks, empty and dry. And then their own lie caught them and they did the very thing they had accused the blacks of wanting to do—they took the women of the other race. They took black women when they had ruined their own. They outraged their own women in one way, and then outraged black women in another."[3]

Thus, the white virgin is clearly part of the black siren syndrome, just as she was an essential to the brute Negro stereotype. She is the Victorian long-suffering wife of the licentious husband who spends his money and affections on kept-women. But with the modern age has come a new view of her: she is more frustrated than self-righteous, more furious than forgiving. Kimbrough sees her as verging on madness. The tone of near-hysteria which dominates much of Southern gothic literature is often allied with sexual frustration and taboo-violation. The black siren at one time represented Negro lust, later she was evidence of Negro primitivism (a charmingly exotic type), but now she has the same sexual desires as the white woman, the same need for affection, the same aversion to abuse. Except that she is more vulnerable, she is no different from a white woman.

Lonnie Coleman's *Clara* is a colorful, well-written little

story of this struggle of the white wife and the black
mistress over the body and soul of the white man. The
white woman's frigid response to her husband drives him
to the arms of their available and affectionate Negro cook,
who has a mulatto child by him and continues to work in
the house, unsuspected by the lethargic and docile white
wife. Eventually the knowledge of the affair (which was
brief and never repeated) is forced on the wife, who is
thereby convinced of what she has long felt: that her
husband is a depraved monster and that Clara, the Negro
cook, is an arrogant hussy. Such a situation usually serves
for tragedy or for melodrama, but Coleman tends to be
realistic and ironically comic in his outlook. The white
wife is too phlegmatic to respond with prolonged energy.
She does not hate the child or the black mother, and she
does not go mad. Rather, she talks out her anger, and then
acts in her own best interests. Husbands are expendable,
but good cooks are hard to find. So after a brief fury, in
which she fires Clara and sends her and the child away, she
rehires the cook-mistress, accepts the incident as ancient
history, and resumes her comfortable life. In time, the
Negro mistress is the only real friend she has. Her husband
dies, still guilt-ridden; the mulatto son dies, and the wife
and the cook spend their old age fussing over the child of
the illegitimate mulatto son. Coleman seems to feel that in
some women lethargy is so dominant that no emotion can
long prevail which might interfere with creature comforts.
Also, most characters in such a situation are emotional,
violent, tragic types. But his heroine has little feeling for
her husband, little concern for social approval, and a
quietly realistic view of life. The story therefore becomes a
comic challenge to the recurrent tragic tale of miscegenation.

Although both Kimbrough and Smith trace the

Southern gynolatry to the myth of Negro lust—and the unspoken fear of retaliation for white lust, the attraction between black men and white women appears minimal. Only a few stories deal with any such attraction. Their usual pattern is to portray the white woman attracted by Negro men as crazy or degenerate (*Sweet Man, Amber Satyr, The Hawk and the Sun, The Horncasters,* for example). When the attraction is real and borders on love (as in *Cinnamon Seed* or *Watch Night*), the girl is too alarmed to take a chance at rousing antagonistic social judgments. So she rejects the man and destroys a part of herself in that action. Hamilton Basso's *Cinnamon Seed* is a particularly sensitive portrayal of the anguish surrounding a black-man-white-woman attraction. The white girl realizing the dangerous affection she feels for a young Negro man, ruins her life by rushing into a loveless marriage that leaves her cold and unfulfilled. And having openly displayed his passion to her, he is so frightened of repercussions that he runs away and stays for ten years. The whole sense of the tempting taboo and the confusion of the couple who understand their own feelings but dare not challenge society makes this an especially powerful story. And the assumption that women will risk misery rather than ostracism is a good reading of human nature.

Sweet Man is a more typical story. The wealthy white female rouee turns to her Negro chauffeur for sexual adventure, enjoying the exoticism of his race and her domination of his masculinity. This corrupt white woman looking for excitement, not for love, is as great a threat to the Negro man as is the young innocent. In this case, she threatens to pretend he has raped her should he try to break off their relationship. The white woman is believable—her desire to dominate, her abuse of power, her need to castrate the male. And the picture of the Negro man also rings true. In his world, the pretense of rape would be fatal for him. His word against hers, his character against hers, his race against hers, his sex against hers—in any category, she would be the preordained victor. Either type of story, that of the man-eating white woman or the loving but rabbit-hearted white girl, has much greater tragic potential than that of the white female sex maniac leaping into bed with a frightened, wide-eyed Negro innocent (*Amber Satyr*) or luring her "Othello" to a tryst in the barn (*The Horncasters*). But any of the scenes can easily serve as the fuse for the lynch story.

Erskine Caldwell, who is not inclined to accept much of Southern mythology, has one of his characters (*In Search of Bisco*) comment that it is fear of having mulatto babies that keeps white women pure. But Lillian Smith suggests an even stronger motive—fear of physical violence. The white man inevitably began to suspect white women of sharing the temptations to which he was so regularly succumbing, and Miss Smith speculates:

Fabulous stories began to be whispered of the Negro male's potency. And as the white man visited more frequently the cabins in the quarters, and stayed more and more away from the big house, his suspicion grew of his wife left alone there with her embroidery and her thoughts. The more he left his sacred statuary while he sought warmer company, the more possessive became his words about her. "Our women" was a phrase that was said more and more glibly. And as suspicion and guilt grew, as minds became more paranoid, they threatened with death any white woman who dared to do what they had done so freely. It is said—I am not certain that it has been proved—that a few white women did cross over the line and paid their penalty and that this penalty of death was dealt them by their own husband or father or brother as the case might be. . . . Southern authorities like Hodding Carter and the late William Alexander Percy have, even in recent years, emphasized the strength of the taboo against white women mating with Negroes, and the heavy penalties exacted of them, at least by the community, though now-adays such women are more often banished than killed; it is the Negro male who receives the death penalty today as a "rapist" when such alliances are discovered.[4]

Harper Lee uses this taboo as the crux of her court case in *To Kill a Mockingbird*. The poor-white girl, lonely and loveless, watches and lusts after a handsome Negro who shows her kindness and offers her help. Lurching at him one day, trying to seduce the innocent-minded black victim, she is surprised by the entrance of her vicious father. In her fright, she protects herself by pretending that the Negro tried to rape her. She can not admit she "tempted a Negro." As Atticus sums up her offense, "She did something that in our society is unspeakable: she kissed a black man. Not an old Uncle, but a strong young Negro man."[5] When the situation is broached in court, it is so outrageous to the jury that they cannot consider the evidence—they must find the Negro guilty. This parallels the somewhat more intricate situation in *Watch Night*. Here the girl cannot admit her affection for her Negro lover, so she accuses him of raping her; and the jury cannot admit a white girl from a good family is morally loose, so they must attribute her pregnancy to rape.

What then of the Negro man in this pattern of interracial temptation? Most novelists do not seem to think that Negro men find white women any more attractive than black except in so far as the alien and forbidden fruit is tempting. Miss Smith has a Negro man in *Strange Fruit* speculate on what it would be like to know a white girl, but only because he is forbidden to communicate with white girls except in the most formal situations and by the most rigidly codified rituals. Elizabeth Spencer goes further by having her Negro man seduce a plain little English girl who finds his blackness appealing, but he does not love her and feels no emotion but pity in remembering the experience. (Baldwin, who falls outside the scope of this study, makes a point of the attraction that white women feel for black men, but he also suggests that the Negro men have only the faintest interest in white women.) Lucy Daniels has her young civil-righter in *Caleb, My Son* date a white girl, not because he finds her tempting (actually her complexion is bad and her hair is bleached to the shade and consistency of straw) but because he needs a symbolic gesture of independence and equality. The only response from the white community is the girl's family's insistence that Caleb marry her. His own family is disgusted that he is bringing shame on them by dating a girl who is not only white but also clearly a slut.

Ralph Ellison has his hero sleeping with white women when he goes North, where miscegenation appears to be neither illegal nor immoral. In the earlier, Southern scenes of *Invisible Man*, a group of young Negro men are forced to watch a white exotic dancer go through her sensual gyrations (with an American flag painted on her rippling belly) without displaying any overt sexual interest—a hideous torture for the boys and a delightful amusement for the men who are watching their reactions. In one contrasting and parallel later scene, when Sybil asks the hero to rape her, he responds by writing a comic message on her belly in lipstick and then is so ashamed of himself that he erases it and pretends he did rape her while she was drunk.

Another time, a woman lures him to her apartment to discuss women's rights, only to prove more interested in brotherhood and sisterhood. Having been tempted to crawl into bed with her against his better judgment, he is alarmed when her husband returns, smiles at them complacently, and goes off to bed after exchanging a few pleasantries. One of the great virtues of Ralph Ellison is his genius for laughing at topics that engender horror, hysteria, or exaggerated nonconcern in lesser artists. While other authors are still focusing their attention on the nature of manliness, Ellison spends his talent on the nature of humanity. His invisible man can only laugh at the vision of himself as a brute Negro. Being a man is not a matter of sleeping with white women or keeping white men from sleeping with Negro women. It is simply a matter of knowing and accepting ones self.

The virtuous-Negro-white-tramp is still not a common theme in Southern literature, but it is becoming less shocking daily. In recent novels we find a pattern ludicrously parallel to that of the Negro female virgins. The ape Negro has now lost so much of his old virility and brutishness that he seems to approach a blonde woman in a bed with embarrassment and repugnance, but with a determination to live up to his racial image, establish his masculine superiority, and to wreak his revenge on the white race.

When, in *Toys in the Attic*, Lillian Hellman has one of her female characters flaunt her Negro lover, she does not even bother providing an extended discussion of the relationship. Miss Hellman is hardly displaying a typical Southern response to this most firmly entrenched of Southern taboos, but even the most Southern of Southerners seem less appalled than formerly. William Faulkner, for example, has his Miss Burden convinced of Joe Christmas' Negroness and becoming his mistress, even calling him "nigger" in the flush of their sadistic-masochistic sex orgies. But then, Miss Burden is a Yankee (or at least descended from Yankees) and is expected to do outlandish things. But poor Joe, who is determined to shock his bedpartners by his Negroness, has some difficulty getting any reaction from any of them. One prostitute brightly

comments, "What about it? You look all right. You ought
to seen the shine I turned out just before your turn came."
Joe turns out to be more easily shocked than the woman,
for the knowledge that a white woman would willingly
sleep with a Negro man nauseates him.

In summary, the miscegenous relationship continues to
appeal to authors who can use it for the cheapest, the most
sensational exploitation. But it also appeals to those who
can use it as the basis for a deep and probing analysis of
Southern mythology and regional thought, delving into
individual drives and conflicts, seeking out the most
significant areas of human action and provoking startled
laughter. The decision to look at one of the opposite sex
and of another race as a human being, rather than as an
object to be used for one's own pleasure; the sensing of
another person's humanity rather than his masklike superficial image—these can be experiences to jar and disturb
the most entrenched Southerner or to enlighten the most
idealistic radical. Jessie Hill Ford allows his conservative
old lawyer to remember the experience of lust turning to
love with a Negro girl, and in that memory to have the
seeds of painful self-knowledge. By no means must the
novel of miscegenous love be simple pornography, as Mr.
Ford's *The Liberation of Lord Byron Jones* clearly
demonstrates.

The old stereotypes that clustered around the theme of
interracial sexual attraction were the brute Negro and the
mulatto mistress. More recently other more subtle types
have appeared: the mammy can be a lusty mistress, the
faithful maid can be a violated innocent, the black cook
can be a loving sensual comforter. On the other side, the
angry young Negro can become the freewheeling lover—the
black Ulysses. Or the Negro man may be a sensitive young
swain pining away for a white love. The white man may be

a brutal poor-white exploiting Negro women or a confused young conformist tempted to break societal taboos. The white woman may be angry or hurt or frustrated or tempted. Thus, the antiquated pattern of Negro brutes lusting after white virgins has broken down: first into an admission of white brutes lusting after Negro virgins, then into an acknowledgement that illicit lust affects a whole group of people and elicits a number of both stock and individual responses. With these new raw materials, so long as the crossing of racial lines is socially and psychologically painful, authors have the raw materials for powerful character studies. In the South, where the taboos and myths are most firmly entrenched, the writers have the most provocative and potentially explosive story lines to exploit. And given the likely continuance of sex as *the* theme in the novel, and illicit sex as increasingly difficult to find in a world of nebulous moral and social codes, the black-white sex life of the South is bound to retain its popularity.

5

MALADJUSTED MULATTOES

If the sociologists and psychologists are right and the Southerner does indeed equate blackness with sensuality, then it is hard to explain why white men choose almost-white mistresses. When an attractive young mulatto walks down the street, the white men turn and leer. Over and over, the Southern novelists have pictured the almost-white Negro girl as in enormous danger from white men. Erskine Caldwell's *A Place Called Estherville* is a poorly written but vivid example of the perils faced by a pretty tan-skinned girl. First she is raped by her white employer. Leaving that job, she finds it almost impossible to find other work. On one rare occasion when she does work, she is attacked by a group of young white boys on her way home. This harassment is interrupted by a white police-man, who also attempts to abuse her sexually. Refusing his advances, she is taken to jail, where her bail is paid by a white man, who later expects her to service visiting salesmen as a favor to him. Eventually, when the rent collector expects sex in return for paying her rent for her, she rebels. It is only fair to say that the girl's brother, Caldwell's parallel example of the white Negro boy, fares even worse in his effort to maintain his virtue in the face of white female lechers. Given the acknowledgement that the Caldwell world is not quite the real world, we still must admit that he does draw from life. And most white and Negro novelists in the South verify his findings—that white men do prefer light Negro girls and do tend to use them as chattels.

This preference may be indicative of the falseness of the blackness-lustiness pattern established in exotic primitive stories, or it may simply mean that white men feel more comfortable with bed mates approximating their racial concepts of ideal beauty. Only recently has there been much effort to acknowledge an alternative to the white criteria for female beauty. Such novels as *Candy* pictured the nappy-haired, coal-black, earth-mother heroine as enormously attractive to Negro males, but white men passed her by without a glance. And even today, in spite of efforts within the Negro community to deny the validity of the white standards that have coaxed Negro girls into torturous efforts with hair straighteners and skin lighteners, blackness is seldom the basis for beauty except in novels by Negro writers. The white man accepts the relativity theory of beauty intellectually, but his emotional and sexual response still conforms to the white ideal. Certainly it would be dishonest for the Southern writer describing Southern life to suggest that any large number of white men feel attracted to darker Negro women, although obviously there was a time when white men used them quite freely for sexual relief.

As a result, mulattoes, quadroons, and octoroons continue to populate Southern novels as mistresses and as victims of violent sexual attacks by whites. Needless to say, the older novels failed to emphasize the possibility of the girl's unwillingness to be the lust object of the white man. Only more recently has this become a standard part of the novel of miscegenation.

On occasion light Negro women even marry white men,

but usually because the white man does not realize the presence of the Negro blood in their veins. Faulkner's Sutpen, who is not especially prejudiced but who does recognize the prejudice of others and the effect that prejudice could have on his life, is married briefly to a woman of mixed blood. After the birth of his son, Charles Bon, Sutpen discovers his wife's ancestry and abruptly leaves her, the son, and the dowry he had formerly coveted. On the other hand, Robert Penn Warren's liberal Yankee hero marries a woman whom he believes to be white (in *Band of Angels*), but does not leave her when he learns of her mother's black blood. However, we are not entirely convinced he would have married her had he known her race before, and she is not convinced that he is unaffected by this knowledge. The irony in such cases as these is that the women have so little Negro blood in their veins that in reality they are white, yet categorized by law and society as Negro. "In some of the southern states anyone with one-eighth or more Negro blood is classed as a Negro; in others, the law prescribes that any trace of Negro blood no matter how remote automatically classes one as a Negro."[1] Whatever the actual state law, Southern society in general classifies Negroes according to the latter pattern; and in order to pass, a mulatto must move out of the community in which he is known, and preferably out of the South that has a long, proud tradition of uncanny ability for spotting the slightest trace of Negro ancestry.

The mulatto has been consistently one of the most popular characters in Southern fiction. The mixture of blood allows the white author to identify more readily with a "Negro" character, and to allow his predominantly white audience to share that identification; it also gives him a chance to discuss differences between the races, to elicit sympathy for society's cruelty to Negroes, and to narrate a tragic tale with social significance. Historically, this has been the purpose of the tragic mulatto—usually a beautiful, almost-white woman, frequently talented in music, often from an aristocratic white family who have passed on to her some of their pride and arrogance. Sterling Brown comments that authors have the *idee fixe* that the Negro of un-mixed blood is no theme for tragedy. Rather, the writer turns to a man or woman without a distinct race, who worships whites but despises and is despised by Negroes.

The tragic-mulatto stereotype, which became popular at approximately the same time as the brute Negro, also served propagandistic purposes: anti-slavery authors used it to counteract the brute-Negro picture. When the story dealt with a light slave, the author usually concentrated on the abuses of slavery: the floggings, the slave mart, the domestic slave trade, forced concubinage, runaways, slave hunts, and persecuted freemen. The mulatto was generally female, nearly white, the product of an illicit union of white aristocrat and slave woman. Brown, a perceptive and defensive Negro critic, is particularly irate at the tacit assumption that any iota of intellect or rebelliousness in the octoroon's nature is an indication of white blood, while any fleshly lusts are clear indications of Negro blood.[2] The stereotyped character has proved herself indestructible, surviving Brown's searing critiques. Manifold tawdry reincarnations of the tragic mulatto populate neo-confederate as well as new-Negro novels, and she has generally retained the whole bundle of cliches.

Hugh Gloster points out that the classic pair of negrophobe novelists, Thomas Nelson Page and Thomas Dixon, portray the character of mixed blood as the "embodiment of the worst qualities of both races and hence as a menace to the dominant group." To them, "the mulatto woman is the diseaser of the white aristocrat, while the mulatto man is the besmircher of white virginity and the dangerous intruder in the political scene."[3]

Most authors reject this approach, however, and are sympathetic in varying degrees to the plight of the mulatto. The possession of Caucasian blood supposedly makes this character the superior of the darker Negro and one with whom the white readers can sympathize. Hence the mulatto, whose rise to become the middle-class Negro with education and taste made him attractive to white middle-class authors, became one of the popular characters in American fiction. It has been in portrayals of this personage that white writers have made their most significant departures from the plantation tradition.[4] Early examples of this tradition are such novels as Cable's *The Grandissimes* (1880) and Mark Twain's *The Tragedy of Pudd'nhead Wilson* (1894). More recent examples, from the Negro renaissance, would include such novels as Jessie Fauset's *There Is Confusion* (1924) and Walter White's *Flight* (1926). Hundreds of good examples, especially since the 'twenties, prove the continuing enthusiasm for what Gloster insists is fundamentally a "color-biased" approach to Negro fiction. He is probably right: certainly the "old familiar mathematic formula" of half-white—reason; half-black—emotion[5] is patently ridiculous. Regardless of its perceptibly antiquated theses, the mulatto stereotype remains the stock basis for the black temptress, the black Christ, and the new Negro.

Several novels appearing in the last forty years have emphasized the curious nature of the miscegenous off-spring. For example, DuBose Heyward's *Mamba's Daughters* explores the climb of a mulatto girl from the degradation of her illegitimate birth and her ghetto home to the society of the wealthy mulattoes of Charleston, and eventually to the artistic aristocracy of New York and the Continent. She finds that the color differentiation serves as the basis for much of the snobbery among the mulattoes, who ape the whites in their music, art, religion, and manners, becoming what Frazier would call "black bourgeoisie" and what Hare would call "black Anglo-Saxons" and what Ellison sees as "white washed." Rejecting this as she has rejected her primitive background, the heroine strives for a balance in her art that can express her divided nature. For a while she fluctuates between the stiffly formal life of the Negro middle-class and the wild temptations of the lusty lower-class, but finally balances her life so that she can feel emotion without shame and use her art without sham.

In Julia Peterkin's *Bright Skin*, the same emphasis upon color and mixed emotions plays a strong part in the decisions of the mulatto girl who is attracted to men of lighter skin, yet married to a "blue gum" Negro; she wants the excitement of the city and the chance for education, yet she is imprisoned in the plantation society that stifles her. The insinuation is that it is her white blood drawing her to a different life, causing her to reject the world of the darker blood. And we feel too that the men who love her are guilty of that same color snobbery we have seen before—they love her for her "bright skin" that makes her different from and more attractive than the black Negroes surrounding her. T.S. Stribling echoes this color snobbery in *The Store*, when the quadroon mother in the story is proud of the white skin of her octoroon son and unhappy in his choice of a dark-skinned wife. Other elements of appearance, such as hair, dress, etc., are also considered more attractive as they approach white ideals.

The more recent novelists have commented on the foolishness of this pattern of color-snobbery, and have admitted that the blackest blue-gum Negro may have psychology as subtle and character as tragic as the lightest Creole. One clear example of the horrors of color snobbery is Barbara Anderson's *Southbound*. The white patron who has been enthusiastic about the young mulatto girl abandons her when the girl reaches puberty and begins to develop distinctly Negroid features. It takes the girl many years and much loneliness to come to terms with herself, accepting her heritage of black and white, and refusing to cater to the tastes of color snobs. At one point, she finds herself tempted to love only that man who has precisely her coloring; when she finds him unwilling to marry a girl no lighter than he, she sees her own foolishness.

But far more powerful than this novel is Peter Feibleman's *A Place Without Twilight*, a penetrating portrayal of a family of light Negroes. Their anger at the neighbors who insult or cultivate them for their color, their fear of outsiders, their over-wrought emotionalism as a result of their plight, reach an hysterical pitch as the mother becomes so obsessed with protecting the children from life that she can be happy only when they are mad or dead. Feibleman is not accepting the stereotyped drives of the whites and the Negroes as the mix in the confused mulatto; he is investigating the human life dominated by fear of both black and white attitudes and frozen into inactivity and finally death by this stultifying fear. His is not a folksy or colorful study of quaint habits and interesting superstitions, but an honest investigation of living creatures.

William Faulkner's Joe Christmas, protagonist of *Light in August*, is another of these thoroughly modern investigations of human motivation. Here Faulkner shows a young man who comes to believe that he is of mixed blood. Without any factual verification of this thesis, he drives himself into a frenzy of hatred for and identification with Negroes. Associating with the Negrophile reformer, Miss Burden, he is tempted to accept the role of the Negro in society. In an agony of self-hatred, he murders her and becomes a "lynch" victim (although not technically a lynch since only one man performs the murder and the subsequent castration). But through all of this, though we are carried along by his conviction of his Negro blood, we are never really certain that it is anything more than a wild fantasy inherited from his maniacal old grandfather. His despair and agony could be nothing more than the self-inflicted wounds motivated by conditioning of a prejudiced society. If there is no Negro blood in Joe Christmas' veins, the whole final meditation on the battle of black blood and white becomes an ironic commentary on Southern mythology.

Faulkner deliberately leaves Joe's racial heritage ambiguous. We tend to believe with him that he has some Negro blood because the children at the orphanage spot it and because the circus owner believes his father was of Negro blood. But the Southerners in the story who are usually proud of their ability to spot the slightest hint of Negroid ancestry are unable to see him as other than "foreign." Since Joe himself insists on telling everyone that he is a Negro, everyone accepts his word. After all, given the Southern attitude toward the Negro, only a madman would admit to Negro blood falsely. (The irony is that we are privy to the suspicion that he is indeed a madman.)

Therefore the responses to him, after his confession, tend to be either strangely disinterested or automatic. The prostitute nauseates him by telling him he is not the first Negro with whom she has slept. Brown is less concerned with his blood than his money. And Miss Burden shows the delight of a perverted liberal who can enjoy her love and her hatred simultaneously—being ravished by him, while calling him Negro, and thrilling at the horror of it all.

People who are really not interested in his race will use it as an instrument to put blame on him or use him as a scapegoat when they themselves are in peril or in the wrong: the dietician turns against him, calling him Negro when he becomes a threat to her security. His young mistress calls him *Negro* when she is forced to flee the town and is party to robbing him. Brown tells the sheriff that he is a Negro when the sheriff is in doubt as to the guilty party in Miss Burden's murder.

But Joe in turn is quite as willing to use the information to hurt others. He meditates on telling his foster mother that she is nurturing a Negro. He delights in telling the women with whom he shares guilty sexual acts. And he hopes to shock Brown with the disclosure. To Joe Christmas, being a Negro is a suspicion with which he can punish himself and shock others. It becomes a necessary tool in his perverse need for flagellation. He is therefore less of a tragic mulatto stereotype than a case study in abnormal psychology.

The community has clearly conceived ideas of what being a Negro means, ideas which Joe shares even though they breed self-hatred in him. When the countryman finds Miss Burden's decapitated body, Faulkner notes that the community hopes that the Negro raped her both before and after the horrible mutilation, thus satisfying the image of the brute Negro. We even suspect that Christmas deliberately chose to conform to this expected Negro violence. Gavin Stevens thinks that the razor is a Negro weapon and sees his flight as a clear indication of his mixed blood.

Black blood drove Joe to the Negro cabin; white blood drew him
out, black blood snatched pistol, white blood wouldn't let him fire
it. "And it was the white blood which sent him to the minister,
which rising in him for the last and final time, sent him against all
reason and all reality, into the embrace of a chimera, a blind faith in
something read in a printed book. Then I believe that the white
blood deserted him for a moment. Just a second, a flicker, allowing
the black to rise in its final moment and make him turn upon that
on which he had postulated his hope of salvation. It was the black
blood which swept him by his own desire beyond the aid of any
man, swept him up into that ecstasy out of a black jungle where life
has already ceased before the heart stops and death is desire and
fulfillment."

Just as his white shirt and dark trousers suggest his
tragically divided role, the white part the rational part, the
black the sensual; so his running to the black neighbor-
hood is the response to his black blood, and his returning
to the white minister indicates the ascendency of his white
blood.

Faulkner refuses to endorse Stevens' reactionary judgment. He refuses to be clear about Joe, just as life refuses
to be clear. Joe's problem is not whether he in fact has
Negro blood. It is not even the equating of Negro with the
dark, fecund, mysterious quality of the female which both
attracts and repells this young perverted-Calvinist. It is a
problem of belonging, feeling a part of a community and a
family. He is not really fretting about whether he is more
black or white, but about which life-style is more
comfortable for him. And his discovery is that neither
satisfies him. This is not a problem of the civil war being
waged inside the tragic mulatto, it is a question of mixed
attitudes—primordial longings in conflict with learned
patterns, unconscious desires in conflict with dictated
hatreds. By mixing Freudian psychology, perverted Calvinism, local prejudices, and racial preconceptions, Faulkner

has created a baroque commentary that is far more complex than any earlier study of the tragic mulatto.

A somewhat more normal, or at least less complex handling of the mixed blood question occurs in Warren's *Band of Angels*. Here Warren explores the more typical fictional problem of an attractive young girl with genteel education and rearing who suddenly discovers at her father's funeral that she is the offspring of a slave. Because of her race, she is bound into slavery and sold. Not only the horror of becoming a chattel, but the whole of her education on the inferiority and unattractiveness of Negroes afflicts her. She is attracted to white men, becoming the mistress of her white owner, and later marrying a young, white Union officer. Her confusion regarding her racial make-up renders her inordinately sensitive to her husband's inadequacies and slights, and eventually drives her to the brink of a love affair with a jet-black Negro she loves, hates, admires, and abuses (the same old temptation known to the Negro siren). She can never quite free herself from her own distaste for the Negro blood inherited through her slave mother. Warren's study is superior to Faulkner's philosophically, for he does explore the nature of love, of racial attitudes, and of self-knowledge. But it does not have the exciting quality of a puzzle put before the reader for him to solve nor the intensity nor the complexity of Faulkner's flawed but powerful novel. Warren conforms more closely to the romantic historical tradition here but is, of course, too good a writer to conform to the usual stereotypes. His heroine resembles the heroine of Elizabeth Coker's *Daughter of Strangers* and others, but Amantha Starr is Warren's own distinct creation. Like Joe Christmas, she is tempted to behave in conformity with the label society gives her; like Joe, she hates the race with which she is

categorized (but with the more delicate response of the
liberally educated rather than the fanatically and barely
educated pattern Joe knew); she too finds the Negro both
attractive and repellent—fascinating because of her identity
with him. But she is by no means so emotional, so given to
violence, so psychologically warped. Consequently, what
Amantha loses in color by being more normal than Joe,
she gains in reality. The story does not have the wild,
uneven quality of *Light in August*. It is a neater, more
believable story. But Faulkner's chaotic vision of the doom
of the South is a more vital and exciting novel to read and
to re-read.

A less psychologically powerful but more romantic
study of the same period and of the same type of person is
Elizabeth Coker's *Daughter of Strangers*, also set in Civil
War days, also involving a young girl reared as white but
actually of mixed blood, who is also sold into slavery when
her father dies, also tempted to become the mistress of her
white owner, and who also recoils from Negro men she
meets from day to day. But her path upward and onward
is clearer than that of Warren's heroine, and we leave her
serving as benefactor of freed slaves, happy with her
educated mulatto husband, satisfied with her role as a free
Negro. Neither Warren nor Faulkner could allow their
heroines or heroes such firmly grounded contentment. We
recognize Miss Coker's story the more romantic handling
of the uplifting tragic mulatto who found herself by
finding a way to serve her people, an echo in fact of
Mamba's granddaughter.

Faulkner, in other stories, uses characters of mixed
blood who have somewhat less violent psychological
problems than Joe Christmas. Charles Bon, with his
quadroon mistress and his love of his own half-sister, is not
so much a study in mixed blood as additional evidence of

the doom of the whole Sutpen brood. If *Absalom!*
Absalom! is in any way a parable of the doom of the
South, then the chapter on Bon parallels the epoch of
rapine and its tragic results. The offspring of the miscegenous union comes back to haunt the establishment
and to threaten the chaste young white virgin with his
desires and his tainted blood. Negro critics tend to regard
Faulkner as excessively alarmed at miscegenation, but he
appears to be more concerned with the sins of sexual abuse
than with the problem of "impure" blood.

Lucas Beauchamp, for example, is less a Negro with
white ancestry or a man with tainted blood than an ornery
McCaslin type. Faulkner is more interested in family traits
than in racial patterns—and in his world a McCaslin
chromosome would cancel out any number of Negro
chromosomes. Lucas is only a Negro when he chooses to
be, and most of the time he chooses not to be one, largely
because it would please too many people for him to
become predictable. Many of the Negroes in Faulkner's
stories have some white blood, and in most cases the
admixture makes little difference in their psychology or
life. The tragedy behind Tomey's, Turl's or Ned McCaslin's
birth is not apparent in the activities of their lives. But
tragedy does appear in the particularly magnificent form
of the heroic old Sam Fathers, who is the son of an Indian
and a mulatto, and is thus the product of three warring,
enslaving, and enslaved races. All three races reject him, or
he them, so that he lives his life out in the woods, the
solitary wise man in the wilderness, without friends,
except the children, and without descendants. Like Ben,
the bear, he achieves heroic stature by his endurance, his
unity with nature, and his eventual death.

Faulkner talks at length about blood and the knowledge
that comes to Sam and others with blood, a discussion that

seems strange to a non-Southerner. This black-blood
fighting white-blood pattern is the closest any Southern
writer has come to a parody of the tragic mulatto theme.
Certainly, as a Southerner, Faulkner may have shared
somewhat in the Southern faith in blood, but it is hard to
credit Gavin Stevens' outrageous commentary of Joe
Christmas' blood as Faulkner's own belief. Southern
communities, by and large, tend to know the whole
history of member families and to believe in the old adage
that "blood tells." From this point of view, blood may be
good or bad, blue or red, black or white. By reflecting on
the family history, the local observer can predict that a
Sartoris will be daring and foolhardy, a Snopes sneaky and
mercenary, and a Sutpen wild and damned—it is in the
blood. This is moderately interesting to those spectators
trying to sort out and categorize elements in the human
drama and is generally a harmless enough activity. But for
an artist to believe completely in the whole scheme of
blood-heritage is restrictive, and it is hard to believe that
Faulkner believed in blood anywhere near as completely as
a man like Gavin Stevens would.

    Some critics feel, however, that the pattern is prejudi-
cial, especially when aimed at Negroes or those with Negro
blood. If heredity is accepted as unchanging and unchange-
able, then the Negro can hardly hope to aspire to become
much more than a hewer of wood and a drawer of water,
or in modern terms, a porter or a bellhop. If not his
progress must lie in the breaking of social and educational
patterns built up by his family and his race. This, however,
need not be at variance with the blood theory since "good
niggers" have often been recognized as more intelligent
and honorable than their fellows, thus hypothetically more
capable of progressing. That a bright house servant sired by
a white "aristocrat" should produce a son who chooses to

become a lawyer is no real refutation of the blood hypothesis.

More damaging is the idea of blood warfare in the products of miscegenation—as if black-white warfare is as inevitable to Southern thinking as capital-labor warfare is to Communist theory. Supposedly the black blood and the white blood stage a gory civil war in the mind and body of the mulatto, much as the medieval writer would have had the Body and the Soul battling it out over possession of Everyman. Certainly, the majority of Southern writers feel that the role of the mulatto is potentially tragic, but the blood conflict theory seldom appears in their discussions. One critic attacks Stevens' speculation on the grotesque murder by Joe Christmas, his reference to the black blood and the white blood battling, first one and then the other claiming ascendency.

"Faulkner, like Paul Green and other Southern writers," explains Irene C. Edmonds, "thinks in terms of an actual war between the white and the black blood in the veins of a person of mixed blood as if there were a struggle between two disparate and infusible elements." She feels that this is the crux of the "tragic mulatto" stereotype, and objects to it: "In reality this assumed conflict represents but another facet of the belief that miscegenation is a mortal sin, and hence there must be some prima-facie evidence to prove its eternal verity. In reality the conflict is between the individual in toto and his environment."[6]

But considering this quotation in the context of the novel and the doubt that we can equate Faulkner with Gavin Stevens here or in *Intruder in the Dust*, we see Faulkner's ironic evasion—the conflict may be nothing more than the explanation the Southern world would impose upon Joe's death, not the actual reason at all.

Faulkner may very well be saying that the conflict is not of blood but of social patterns. Since society demands one code of behavior from the white man and an entirely different one from the Negro, it is virtually impossible for anyone to adapt himself to both codes. The consequent dichotomy then is socially or environmentally imposed and is not innate. The man of mixed blood belongs with no clan, he is isolated. This is true even if he only believes that he has the dual heritage, and it is the real reason for the continuing interest in the tragic mulatto. In his aloneness, he has become a symbol of modern man and his terrifying impotence in an alien and unfriendly universe. He is rootless, imageless, forced to create a personality and a heritage—much as the Negro or the American or the modern anywhere.

As evidence of Faulkner's perceptiveness, contrast him with Allen Tate who says of his tragic mulatto, Yellow Jim, in *The Fathers*, "white blood may have ruined poor Yellow Jim in the end. He knew what his blood was and he had many of the feelings of a white man he could never express. He had conscience and pride, and no man, whatever his hue may be, can have more." Note here the condescending tone of Tate and his suggestion that conscience and pride are exclusively characteristic of the white race—a clear contrast to Faulkner's less prejudiced treatment of the Negro. Tate accepts the thesis that the fruits of miscegenation are potentially tragic—the standard argument against interracial sexual intercourse.

Other Southerners concur on the isolation and maladjustment of the mulatto. Julia Peterkin calls "bright skins" "no nation bastards." And Peter Feibleman insists they are hated by both blacks and whites. Whites push light Negroes harder, he comments, as if to underline the separation from them. And Negroes tend to treat them as if they are white, especially when they are angry; they find them perfect scapegoats on whom they can relieve their aggressions in lieu of the offending but impregnable whites.

But outside of their clashing blood and their social isolation, fictional mulattoes also have psychological confusion, an awareness of the absence of tradition or position or proper codes of behavior. Taught to hate the very thing that they are, they can find no peace and no security. Elizabeth Spencer has one of her characters explain how the mulatto looks to a white man: Jeems, in *Fire in the Morning*, has just puzzled the whole community by shooting a white man. A commentator says:

Explain these bastard white niggers if you can. They stop me cold. They'll walk through the streets like a white man and they'll come do business with you just pushing the line of the way a white man stands, talks and moves his hands, and it's not something that makes me mad and arrogant, as much as it makes me plain nervous. There it stands and what is it? Because five minutes after he leaves you, he'll mix up with an honest-to-God nigger in a scrape that's got the stamp of the colored race marked over it from start to finish, but often pushing the line even there in an exaggeration of violence. I've sometimes thought that day and night might make the difference. A white man under the sun, and under the roving night a Negro again. But I don't know.

There can be no doubt about the literary interest in the "white nigger" character. When the mulatto is not a main character, he or she still serves well as a shadowy minor character. Joe David Brown, for instance, uses a typically beautiful sensitive mulatto as the crucial issue in his war novel, *Kings Go Forth*. Needing an excuse for his two soldiers to hate each other and plan to kill one another, he drags out a beautiful mulatto, lets her fall in love with one of the soldiers and the other fall in love with her. Then he has the one (predictably the bigoted Southerner) seduce her, abandon her, and precipitate her suicide. The other soldier, who loves her, must now avenge her cruel death. But the mulatto girl is clearly the old stereotype dusted off for use in a tough war novel.

Or there is Frances Gaither who finds the yellow offspring of a debased overseer a handy symbol of the injustices of the plantation system, but related to the action of her novel (*Follow the Drinking Gourd*). And there is Edith Pope who in *Colcorton* uses the secret of mixed blood as the basis of the novel's suspense and the key to its mystery. Eventually, we understand the heroine's deliberate celibacy and her dismay at her brother's marriage and the announcement of his wife's pregnancy— she had hoped to keep the mixed blood from continuing into another generation. Mulattoes populate such novels as *The White Band, Nigger, Chain in the Heart, Courthouse Square, Cinnamon Seed,* and hundreds of others.

Some of the best of the mixed-blood stories are, of course, Faulkner's *Light in August* and *Intruder in the Dust,* as well as his collection of Negro stories *Go Down, Moses*; Warren's *Band of Angels,* Shirley Ann Grau's *Keepers of the House,* and Peter Feibleman's *Place Without Twilight.* These stories, like many of the others, touch on such problems as passing, color snobbery, prejudice, etc., but not as if these problems were the whole point of the tale. Shirley Ann Grau, for example, is capable of making us see deeply into the atrophied heart of a disillusioned woman. The heroine's lust for vengeance has Greek ferocity, so that when she taunts her half-brother with the threat that she may one day reveal his parentage to his unsuspecting white wife, we are less concerned with her attitude toward mulattoes and the problem of miscegenation than we are with her declining humanity. The brother deserves whatever she decides to dole out to him, but she is rapidly drying up her own soul as she metes out her justice.

Or Robert Penn Warren concerns us with such problems as the nature of freedom and the horror of self-hatred. Is love a crueler bond than force, he asks. Human life, after all, is more complex and exciting than would be suggested by analysis of humanity only in reference to skin color. Faulkner may well prove to be the wisest of the lot by presenting one mulatto who refuses to act by anyone's code—black or white—and another who destroys himself by accepting society's evaluation of him. Joe Christmas, for the very mystery of his blood, may be the best of the artistic products of miscegenation; for after all the real problem is not the blood itself but man's attitude toward it. This social diagnosis is clearly a more penetrating evaluation than the old war-of-the-races theory which is still depressingly popular.

Obviously, the mulatto will persevere in Southern fiction for some time to come. He is indispensable to a literature that reflects the area, its taboos and myths, its fears and lusts, its shame and its burdens. The mulatto is the only-too-obvious badge of white abuse of the Negro, of the hidden anguish of the system of slavery, of the continuing hypocrisy in racial attitudes. He is a familiar mystery to the Southerner, the bar sinister of his family, his servant and his brother, a man of his own race whose whole life is alien and enigmatic to the white man. As such, the man or woman of mixed blood opens a whole series of interesting questions that the perceptive author is tempted to explore: to what extent is the Negroness in the mulatto beautiful; what is the mulatto's real emotion toward her white lover-employer; how does the white man respond to the sense of the broken taboo; which racial tradition does the mulatto embrace? Thus, he can be symbolic of the modern search for tradition, for identity, for loyalties, and for communication. The horror of aloneness is the spine of the new tragic mulatto. He need not be the brilliant-but-abused character of the Harlem renaissance. More often, he is a subdued, sensitive man searching for a way to make himself visible—not so much tragic as maladjusted and displaced. The tradition-bound, unthinking writer may still use the stereotype to perpetuate the old mythologies and prejudices. But through the character of mixed racial background, the good author can comment on the American dream, the shallowness of conventional attitudes, the existential problem of defining oneself—in short, on modern man.

THE BLACK CHRIST

"It is instructive that Hemingway, born into a civilization characterized by violence, should seize upon the ritualizing violence of the culturally distant Spanish bullfight as the laboratory for developing his style. For it was, for Americans, an amoral violence (though not for the Spaniards) which he was seeking. Otherwise he might have studied that ritual of violence closer to home, that ritual in which the sacrifice is that of a human scapegoat, the lynching bee. Certainly this rite is not confined to the rope as agency, nor to the South as scene, nor even to the Negro as victim."[1]

In this comment Ralph Ellison points to the universal and artistic qualities of the "lynching bee." It is a ritual of violence indeed, a ritual which in the South is most often aimed at purging the community of a dangerous personality—usually a man of mixed blood, and generally as a result of sexual threat (real or supposed) to a white woman. The ritual is certainly allied with the archetypal scapegoat pattern, and is often clearly symbolic of the sacrifice of Christ himself.

The background of this macabre practice in the South is clearly established in numerous studies of Southern history and custom. W.J. Cash describes the rationale for the early choice of Negroes as lynch victims in his classic study of

Southern thought, *The Mind of the South*. After discussing
the Southerners' rape complex, he continues:

> . . . they justified—and sincerely justified—violence toward the
> Negro as demanded in defense of woman, and though the offenses of
> by far the greater number of the victims had nothing immediately to do
> with sex.
>
> The second great sanction for violence which the Yankee had
> created was this: That, quite apart from the woman question, and in
> sober reality, he had made it virtually necessary. Stripped for a
> decade of all control of its government, stripped for three decades of
> the effective use of that government to the ends it willed, the South
> was left with scarcely any feasible way to mastery save only this one
> of the use of naked force; perhaps with no other one, if we take the
> character of the people into account.
>
> And here once more it was the Negro who was the obviously
> appointed scapegoat. For in addition to being the immediate fact at
> issue, he was the only really practical victim. To horsewhip, to tar,
> to hang a particularly obnoxious carpetbagger or scalawag, to reach
> even, as it happened once at Yanceyville in North Carolina, into the
> very carpetbag courtroom and snatch such a fellow away to the
> doom he deserved—all of this might be very fine and satisfying, but
> it plainly could not be carried out on any extended scale. These men
> were mainly in a position to be easily protected, could be got at only
> at an impossible risk and at the cost of certain recognition soon or
> late, Klan disguise or no Klan disguise; at the cost, eventually, of
> counter-hangings. On the other hand, to give the black man the
> works was just as effectively to strike Yankeedom, to serve notice
> of the South's will; terrifying him into frozen silence was easy; and
> in the world there were not bayonets enough to guard all the cabins
> scattered through this wide land.[2]

Cash here attributes the inception of mob action against
the Negro to a combination of sex-fear (that old myth of
the Negro's enormous sexual appetite for white women
and unspoken fear of the Negro man's retaliation for the
white man's use of Negro women); the hatred of the
Yankees and the defeat suffered at their hands; and the

need for justice or vengeance. These are usually the reasons that appear in literature as well as in life, although the novelist of the modern era finds the more benign motives suspect. And even the sexual fear is interpreted in the post-Freudian era as sex envy instead.

Early novelists, such as Dixon, saw terror as essential to control the brute Negro. But few authors have felt the burst of patriotic zeal at the merest glimpse of the Klan that Dixon appears to have experienced. And even negrophobe Dixon did not really approve of lynching. Cash says that by 1900, most of the upper-class whites were growing uneasy about the custom and were developing a contempt for "nigger-hate" and "nigger-hazing"—setting up thereby the convention that only white-trash indulged in such amusements. Gradually, as the more responsible citizens withdrew, the whole mob action became more sadistic. "From the 1880's on, as Walter White has accurately pointed out, there appears a waxing inclination to abandon such relatively mild and decent ways of dispatching the mob's victim as hanging and shooting in favor of burning, often of roasting over slow fires, after preliminary mutilations and tortures—a disposition to revel in the infliction of the most devilish and prolonged agonies."[3] Needless to say, the authors have made free use of this aspect of the lynch scene, since sadism invariably makes colorful literature and effective social protest. In recent years, although the custom of the lynch party has declined, it has not entirely disappeared. Therefore an author need not limit his scene to Reconstruction days in order to justify the inclusion of a lynch or near-lynch. In fact, judging from the tone of Southern novelists, most of the South is perpetually primed for a good lynching bee, simply waiting an excuse to begin. Any unrest can bring on a new rash of lynchings, and many authors, as well as civil authorities, feel that the Supreme Court decisions on integration and the new Civil Rights legislation may precipitate new violence. Others have commented that, on the contrary, the New South may well see a decrease in violence. And recent trends in Negro political and social action have suggested a complete reversal in time of the pattern of the Negro as helpless victim.

Artistically, the lynch has been a useful tool for climaxing the story, for providing suspense, for precipitating the "moment of truth" or the recognition scene, as an excuse for revelling in gothic horrors and fanatical sadism, or as a means to make the story heroic, universal, frightening, or even ironic. It is easy to determine a man's view of human nature, of the South, and of the Negro race from his attitude toward the lynch or the threat of lynch. Walter White uses lynch scenes to preach against the grotesque custom; Arthur Gordon uses the lynch as a commentary on Southern savagery; Harper Lee uses the averted lynch as a tribute to men's good sense and children's innocence; Elizabeth Spencer uses it once as an ironic commentary on the new Negro and once as the basis for revealing men's weakness before an effective leader; William Faulkner uses it once for the fear it engenders, another time for the ironic motives it reveals, and still again to give symbolic implications to a man's death; Richard Wright uses it to show the cruelty of whites and heroism of victimized blacks. While Miss Spencer prefers to write around lynching, since a lynch scene would interfere with the ironic intellectuality of her tone, Faulkner delights in indulging in the nightmare effects and detailed horrors of the actual lynching.

No author of any stature condones it. Most are as critical of this practice as they are of the white rape of

Negro women. And most oppose lynching for the same
reasons that Odum cited in 1931:

> Lynching attains none of the ends for which it has been defended. It
> proves no superiority. It clarifies no issues. It brings no happiness. It
> adds nothing to the richness of human living or the development of
> social personality. It accentuates devastating fear. It sets the
> folkways over against the stateways in lawless revolt. It cheapens
> human life and lessens respect for human liberty and personality. It
> defeats the ends of justice. It violates all the better traditions of
> Southern honor and ideals. It sets the strong brutally over against
> the weak. It negates the South's claim for excellence and genius in
> the science of politics. Its cost is frightful in money and in men. It
> drains off energies and resources. It blackens the reputation of every
> state. It cripples a race and handicaps a region. It intensifies racial
> animosities, isolates a section, sets people against people, and retards
> a wholesome integration of national culture.[4]

(Notice, incidentally, in this listing of sinister effects, that
the salvation of mankind is not included as a possible
offsetting value—and this makes the Christ analogy somewhat dissatisfying.)

One of the most vocal lynch opponents among the
novelists has been Lillian Smith, who uses the lynching of
an innocent Negro as the climactic scene of *Strange Fruit*.
The murder of the white man (the lover-rapist of the
Negro heroine described earlier) that precipitated the
lynching was indeed involved with sex: in this case, the
Negro murderer (the girl's brother) is retaliating for the
white man's rape of a Negro woman—just the opposite of
the classic excuse for the lynch. But Miss Smith feels that
the crowd's anger at the murder of a white man does not
fully explain the lynching of the Negro murder suspect. It
is also the unrest resulting from the war and the
subsequent labor problems that the South is experiencing.
In her more forthright explanation included in *Killers of*

the Dream, she explains her version of lynch psychology more fully. The lynchers are not real killers as a rule, and the Negro is an anonymous victim. But the riddling of the body with bullets, with each person in the group killing the lifeless body again and again suggests to her that "the lynched Negro becomes *not an object that must die* but a receptacle for every man's damned-up hate, and a receptacle for every man's forbidden sex feelings." (Note the echo of Cash's reasoning.) "Sex and hate," she continues, "cohabiting in the darkness of minds too long, pour out their progeny of cruelty on anything that can serve as a symbol of an unnamed relationship that in his heart each man wants to kill and befoul. That, sometimes, the lynchers do cut off the genitals of the lynched and divide them into bits to be distributed to participants as souvenirs is no more than a coda to this composition of hate and guilt and sex hunger and fear, created by our way of life in the South, and by our families and ideas of right and wrong."[5] So Lillian Smith sees the lynching ritual as a sort of Dixie version of the old Bacchic rites.

Other authors have made equally vitriolic comments on the motivation for white violence against innocent Negroes, but more dramatically expressed. Ellen Glasgow, for instance, who seldom uses Negroes in a focal position of her stories, fixed briefly on a scene where two white men plan to castrate a young Negro boy for simply jostling a white woman on the street (in *Virginia*). And Emma Godchaux shows a brutal white man killing a Negro because he blows his horn every evening ("The Horn That Called Bambine" in *Southern Harvest*). Attaway's *Blood on the Forge* shows a Negro lynched for stumbling into a white woman in broad daylight.

Technically, these are not all lynchings because they are not all the work of mobs, just as the death of Joe

Christmas is not a lynching. But, when the society supports the actions, and when the Negro has no sanctuary nor recourse against such violence from whites, the technical difference seems insignificant to the reader and certainly to the victim. The lynch scene with the whole mob ranting and crying for blood does make a more dramatic scene, but the private acts of violence are more common in literature—and undoubtedly in life. Slaughter of innocent Negroes by berserk whites, not by a mob, occurs for instance in Spencer's *Voice at the Back Door* and Warren's *Brother to Dragons*.

The most frequent perpetrators of such atrocities are rednecks and policemen. The question of police brutality is very old and very common to the Southern writer, who has for years been aware of the lop-sided legal system and the potential for police abuse of power. Jessie Hill Ford's recent novel, *The Liberation of Lord Byron Jones*, modernizes the scene by having his sadistic policeman procure confessions by applying electric cattle prods to Negro men's testicles and Negro women's breasts. He shows the abuses possible because of the Negroes' fear of the law: the false arrests and the extortion, the sexual abuse of Negro women, even the murder and mutilation of a Negro litigant. Carson McCullers, in *The Heart Is a Lonely Hunter*, protests the brutality of the chain gang; one of her characters is chained in an icy cell so that his feet freeze and must be amputated.

Authors emphasize not only the cruelty of the law officers themselves, but their permissiveness toward the viciousness of other whites. Forcing an old Negro woman to roast alive in her burning house which a mob has set ablaze (in *Straw in the South Wind*), vandalizing of Negro businesses (in *Reprisal*), beating of a Negro who refused to act decorously on a bus (in *Winds of Fear*), the burning of

Negro homes (in *The Horncasters*) and of a whole Negro district (in *Courthouse Square*), and all the other countless examples of rapes, whippings, beatings, and mutilations ignored by the police but exploited by modern realistic and naturalistic writers—these all make the life of the Negro in modern fiction look like hell on earth.

In addition to all these Zolaesque possibilities are the abuses of the legal system itself as administered in the South, which the more legalistic and less gothic novelists may prefer to explore. The Southern judicial system with its typical all-white jury breeds injustice in three ways: "1) Negroes committing crimes against Negroes are likely to be let off too easily; 2) Negroes committing crimes against whites receive unduly harsh penalties; 3) whites committing crimes against Negroes either get off scot free or receive token sentences."[6] Yet most Southern writers are staunch advocates of a just legal system (as is Faulkner, for example) and many see that the failure of the jury system can easily be the greatest injury wrought by current injustice to the Negro. The Southerner tends to be committed to the ideals of law, in spite of a basic violence in the society: T.S. Stribling has found this an especially ludicrous part of Southern thought; Faulkner hopes that we may emerge from the whole racial conflict with some respect for the law still intact, though he is afraid we will not, and Harper Lee puts her faith in the good will of men of law, the gradual evolution of values, and the erosion of prejudice.

To a number of authors, the Negro victim is far more than a symbol of injustice. In a few cases, his death means something to the community or at least to certain members of the community—something that might eventually evolve into the means for their salvation. While the death of the Negro in Harper Lee's novel is senseless—like the meaningless and gratuitous destruction of a mocking-bird—still it breeds shame in the community and plants the seeds of change. Paxton Davis takes a more heroic view of his Negro in *Two Soldiers*: he allows him consciously to elect death, a necessity if he is to be a tragic hero rather than a tormented and animalistic victim. The Negro soldier has murdered a white man (an act of fear rather than of hate) and has escaped his pursuers to find a life with meaning and happiness among some primitive peoples in the jungles of Asia. But he chooses to leave the new-found life, to help his wounded enemy, and to return to his death in order that his life may have significance. A more heroic version of Bigger Thomas (who is more the victim than the hero of *Native Son*), this black Lord Jim is willing to die in order to prove he is a man. A Negro character in a short play by Paul Green anticipated the heroism of Paxton's black soldier: Green's Herculean black woodsman deliber-ately sacrifices himself to the mob in order to save his fellows, becoming more precisely a Christ symbol than is usual in literature. So is Faulkner's Nancy Mannigoe in *Requiem for a Nun* willing to die to redeem her own life and the lives of those she loves. The governor refuses to grant her a pardon for the murder of Temple Drake's small baby, because he believes she has the right to sacrifice her worthless, debased life: good can come out of evil, we are told, and suffering is a way of salvation.

Nancy is the most successful Christ symbol among Faulkner's Negro characters, even though others approx-imate the role. Joe Christmas' very name should allow ample scholarly debate as to whether Joe is really Jesus (see C. Hugh Holman, "The Unity of Faulkner's *Light in August*,"[7] for example), and plenty of analogies between their lives are available: They both have mysterious origins, humble births, simple childhood experiences among relig-

ious working people. They both start the active part of
their lives at thirty, they both are homeless wanderers.
They both end with jails, mobs demanding their punishment, and violent deaths. But since Joe is a bootlegger, a
murderer, a rapist, and a latent homosexual, the analogy is
at best inexact. However Nancy might also be considered
less than an unblemished sacrificial offering—she was a
dope-addict and prostitute before her stay with Temple.
Yet Faulkner sees her as a nun. So whether or not we see
Joe Christmas as a black Christ (since he may not be black
and he is only ironically Christ), we must see his death as
symbolic and significant. As the Negro is psychologically
lynched and castrated by his community, so Joe is
physically murdered and castrated by the fascist Percy
Grimm. "We lynch the Negro's soul every day of our
lives," says one of Smith's characters in *Strange Fruit*. Miss
Burden sees a black shadow in the shape of a cross falling
over all the people, and she believes there is no escape
from this shadow. "But in order to rise," her father tells
her, "you must raise the shadow with you." In a strange
speech, he continues, "The curse of the black race is God's
curse. But the curse of the white race is the black man who
will be forever God's chosen own because He once cursed
him." In this we see Joe as one of God's chosen as well as a
part of the cross whose shadow disturbs the white South.

Faulkner is clearly superior to the great majority of
Southern writers who have used Christ symbolism in their
fiction. He perpetrates a macabre union between a perverse
form of Calvinism, a lust for violence, a Freudian obsession
with sex, and archetypal patterns of recurrence, sacrifice,
and renewal to express the complex nature of Southern
cruelty. In a world of angry memories, ferocious feuds,
possessive love of the land, warped philosophies, and
deeply imbedded prejudices, no rational solutions count

for much. There is no easy explanation for Joe's murder of Miss Burden or Percy Grimm's murder of Joe. Lucas Beauchamp, realizing the baroque patterns of Southern prejudice, makes no effort to explain his actions to the furious crowd. He uses white men to work his exoneration for him, allowing them to discover the truth for themselves, refusing to involve himself in useless arguments or expose himself to needless hostility. Lucas is particularly interesting in that he is never confused about the nature of the Negro or the white man, and is able to use other people's blindness against them. He would never follow the path of a Joe Christmas because he is too wise and too eager to survive.

Actually, the young victim of "Dry September" is the most precisely symbolic of the Faulkner Christ-figures. The story follows more carefully the ritualistic design of the Southern lynchings, to the extent that it becomes the paradigm for lynch stories. Caldwell's short stories dealing with lynch conform to this pattern, differing in their greater brutality and less effective mood.

For a while there was a mania for Christ-lynch stories of which Waldo Frank's *Holiday* is the most poetic and obvious. His hero, John Cloud, is lynched in Nazareth by a crowd fresh from revival services who believe he has raped a white girl named Virginia. Mary and his mother are beside him as he goes to this tragic death. At the end of the day his fair bronze body has melted in the fire. The town peers with grimed eyes through the murk of its spent lust. Virginia (still a Virgin) sleeps innocently in her bed, and the ship *Psyche* stands at an empty pier, pointing from Nazareth out into the world.

Other stories draw equally obvious analogies to Christ: Vernon Loggins' "Neber Said a Mumblin' Word" describes the lynch of a deaf-and-dumb Negro while echoing the spiritual, "Dey pierced Him in de side,/An He neber said a mumblin' word." Byron Reech, in *The Hawk and the Sun*, catches the ritualistic quality of the lynch with the classic build-up, the news of the pseudo-rape, the selection of the victim, the gathering of the mob, the gestures of conscience-stricken, inept men of good will, the sacrifice, and the aftermath. His people are all symbolically named and all speak their parts in the ritual formally and properly. The minister likens Dandelion, the crippled victim, to Stephen and Christ—to the scapegoat of the Israelites—who must be offered to the gods of evil and destruction, gods who are living but nowhere enshrined except in the hearts of men.

In a sense, the lynch in Southern fiction is a reinforcement of the demand for Negro conformity. The first Negro to try to register his child in a white school, the first one to go to work in a white plant, the first to sit at the front of the bus, the first to paint his shack white—these are the candidates for victimization. It is increasingly a conscious choice on the part of the victim, as we see in such a story as *A Good Man*, by Jefferson Young, who tells of a Negro's desire to have a white house, no matter what the monetary, social, or psychological expense. The perils of death at the hands of the mob are less today than previously, though the danger of private violence is still very real. Jefferson's wife is too frightened to let her husband paint their house, although it is doubtful that the couple are in mortal peril. But the election of martyrdom is becoming increasingly less heroic as safeguards enter, and the role of the Negro as the Christ is currently less popular than in the years between the world wars.

The white characters in such stories are usually as stereotyped as the Negroes. If he broadcasts his challenge, Joe Christmas will usually find his Percy Grimm. While the

Negro is usually a mulatto, Apollo-like in appearance, by
nature independent and intelligent, his family (if he has
one—he is often a loner) is fearful, less well educated, and
helpless. There are occasional cases of revenge such as in
Arthur Gordon's *Reprisal* or Richard Wright's tale of the
old mother who managed to kill several of the lynchers by
hiding a gun in her son's shroud (in "Bright and Morning
Star" from *Uncle Tom's Children*). Usually the Negroes
scatter, huddling out of sight until the violent emotions are
spent. The lynchers, all white, are drunks, red-necks,
illiterates, wastrels, and fascist fanatics; the law officers are
either variations of these same poor-white types or else
heroic, rational servants of the law; the moderates are the
ineffectual middle-class who prefer to recoil in horror and
then forget about the whole sorry mess; the heroes are the
aristocrats who can control mobs (Northern liberals
generally prove as inept as the moderates) or
"innocents"—free-thinking women and children.

A perfect example of the stereotyped pattern is found
in Douglas Kiker's *The Southerner*. Here an intelligent and
attractive young Negro couple decide to enroll their child
in a previously all-white school; a sharp-tongued, realistic
newspaper man (with a heart of gold, naturally) tries to
dissuade them; an aggressive new Negro attorney grimly
goes ahead; a mob of white rabble gathers to "get" the
Negro hero and his family; the newspaper man tries to stop
the make-shift Klan group; but it is the handsome, young,
debonair Southern aristocrat who actually performs the
feat and sends them on their shame-faced way. Note the
only break in the story pattern is the introduction of the
new Negro who is educated and aggressive, but who is also
becoming stereotyped, and there is also an angry crowd of
Negroes who refuse to vacate the streets in the usual way,
a new touch in fiction.

Th e pattern does, in fact, become so predictable that it is a pleasure to hear one of Spencer's characters parody it in *Voice at the Back Door*: Kerney and Duncan are speculating on the possibilities of a lynch mob gathering to "get" the Negro in the jail; Kerney tells Duncan that he expects no outbreak of violence—"These things are supposed to happen in the middle of September after it hasn't rained for forty weeks, after all the cattle have died of thirst and their stench rolls in from the country and there's so much dust the sun looks bloody all day long." It is too cold, it has been raining too hard, and it is the wrong time of year for a lynching. But then, admits Kerney, all he knows about lynchings is what he has read in Faulkner.

Clearly the character of the black Christ is becoming passee. In stories about Reconstruction days, or accounts of post-World War I lynchings, he still figures. But in the modern South, the practice of mutilation and murder has been declining in popularity probably, in part, because authors such as Caldwell and Faulkner and Wright have encouraged sympathy for the lynch victim and horror at the mob's psychology. So long as Southern authors are honestly describing the sinister kink in the brains of otherwise decent people, the psychology of the lynchers has been interesting. But as the villain appears more and more often as a Percy Grimm, he becomes no more than an unthinking, totally depraved villain. More often now, the lynch or the mob violence is pictured by a horrified noncombatant who is shocked at the human capacity for lunacy. This undoubtedly serves a commendably moral, social purpose; but the value of the resultant fiction is negligible. One of the great difficulties involved in working with great archetypal patterns such as sin and sacrifice is that ritual seems pretentious in modern literature as in modern life. In an age that prefers realism and individualism, the great lumbering sacrificial rite is incongruous.

If, on the other hand, the author can bring new interpretations to bear on the topic, or bury the ritual beneath common appearances, or explain the complex motives of the participants, he has some hope of success. Unfortunately, most authors approach the black Christ with more sincerity than ability and most of the resultant novels have proven less than immortal.

In stories dealing with the new Negro, occasional threats of mob violence figure crucially in the tale, but authors hesitate to insist on the whole machinery of the Christ symbolism. The reaction of man in the face of possible death is as useful to the Southern novelist as it has been to Hemingway. Sometimes, the Negro turns and runs, sometimes he stays and dies, but more often he stays and talks and wins. The Negro, seen as a type of man and not as a stereotyped victim, may now react in numerous ways—one of which may be the election of a meaningful death. But in recent novels, if men shoot at the Negro hero, he brings them to trial; if they threaten him, he calls their bluff. He may lose, but only by an error in judgment.

So long as the Klan rides and so long as Negroes are victims of mob action, the black Christ will remain an available and potentially effective stereotype and will be accompanied by his assorted cluster of black and white stereotyped associates. But as the new Negro emerges, the lamb will bleat less pitifully and helplessly on the sacrificial altar; lynchers will be less impervious to judicial rein and punishment, and the black Christ will sink into oblivion joining Sambo and Uncle Tom in the limbo of discarded Negro stereotypes. Violence, Cash tells us, is inherent in the mind of the South, but the ritual of the lynch is not the only means of indulging it. Artists can find suitable gothic horrors in individual violence; it may have less symbolic delight, but it also lends itself somewhat less to stereotyping.

7

THE BLACK PROLETARIAN

In Reconstruction and early twentieth-century Southern fiction, the role of the Negro was fairly uniform. He was generally a grinning background figure, seldom a central character, interesting exclusively for his impingement on white lives. Until local colorists saw in him material for exotic primitive stories, he was rarely pictured in his native habitat. Nor, considering the usual life of the Southern Negro, was there much reason for lingering to consider him. His existence was severely circumscribed: he worked long hours for small pay; he lived in an unpainted, run-down shack; his meals were left-overs from white tables or fatback and cornbread—the staples he knew and could afford. His clothes were ragged; his pleasures were sexual, alcoholic, or social. His religion was fanatic. In short, he lived a life focused on present joy supported by hopes of future fulfillment. His aspirations for this life were generally limited to his opportunities within Southern rural serfdom. The Negroes who wanted education and advancement either moved away or ended as lynch victims or cynical Uncle Toms. The North and the city were, to most Southern Negroes, almost mythical places, dreamed of but largely unknown. Escape North seemed almost as difficult to them as it had to ante-bellum slaves.

Thus, unless the author was inclined to mordant naturalism, social protest, or local color, there was little in the life
of the average Negro to appeal to his imagination. And for
the most part, Southern novelists have been romantics
rather than realists. While Northern authors were describing
the new industries and the growing urban problems around
them, the Southerners were content to dream of the old
days. Only a rare social critic like Ellen Glasgow dared to
look directly at the life around her and comment on it. But
even Miss Glasgow seldom looked deeply into the plight of
the Negro, content instead to smile sardonically at the
mythology surrounding white lives in the South.

The first World War interrupted the long reverie of
Southern artists and forced them to adopt new ideas and
new forms. For the first time, large numbers of Southern
Negroes were able to see something of life outside the
South. And many came home sounding like Faulkner's
Caspey (in *Sartoris*)—aware of better opportunities and less
need for servility in other parts of the world. "I don't take
nothin' fum white folks no more," Caspey mutters belliger-
ently. Many other Southern Negroes echoed his tone,
although like him most had been restricted in their wartime
service to menial duties. Even though Caspey brags of his
valor, he had little opportunity to do more than unload
freighters—most of the Negroes who served in the war
found their roles parallel to their roles in peacetime.

But while Faulkner's Negro veteran proves to be nothing
more than a lazy buffoon, many others benefited from
their glimpse of an alternate life. Not all were so satisfied as
Caspey to relinquish the advantages they had gained in the
war years. Clement Wood's *Nigger* paints a much harsher
picture of the post-war South and the brutal treatment of
returning Negro veterans: the violence, the rejuvenation of
the Klan, the exodus to the North—none of which is

apparent in Faulkner's world. Fear was aroused in Southern
hearts as Negro veterans returned dressed like white men,
having won medals for killing white men overseas, and
often having slept with white women. A minor character in
Stribling's *Birthright* is a returning Negro veteran who is
dissatisfied with the Southern world to which he returns.
His discontent quickly lands him first in jail and subse-
quently in the graveyard.

Actually, after the war, there was not so much racial
strife as the South had feared, but there was a new problem
to face: industry needed laborers to supply the booming
economy. Turning South to tap the enormous supply of
cheap Negro labor, the industrialists offered the Negroes
wages that looked astronomical by comparison with their
bare subsistence earnings as share-croppers. *A Wind Is
Rising, High John the Conqueror,* and *Blood on the Forge*
all picture the economic and psychological distress that
drove men from Southern farms to northern industry. In
these stories, as in life, the share-croppers find that their
efforts go unrewarded. The "furnish" keeps them on the
verge of survival and prevents them from either progressing
or changing. They are trapped in a pattern of perennial
serfdom, tied to the land and to heartless landowners.
There is no recourse in law for their complaints; they are
consistently cheated in stores and robbed by whites.
Attractive Negro women are natural victims for lecherous
white men, and Negro men dare not defend their wives or
daughters for fear of their own lives. Education is discouraged and serves as an irritant to white people who
prefer their Negroes ignorant. Negro croppers own no
property, have almost no leisure, have no hopes for their
children's greater prosperity in the South, and die young
and unnoticed. When they are sick or old, they are
discarded like the peeling of an orange. The lot of many of

the Negro share-croppers, as pictured in the more depressingly naturalistic novels and short stories, makes
mockery of sentimental attachment to paternalism.

The promise of better social, economic, and educational
conditions made the North appear a virtual Canaan to the
Southern Negro; so the great migration began—a migration
that was to change the whole face of the country and the
whole situation of the Negro. To the horror of the South,
one-half million Negroes poured North in the war years,
and the flow continued afterwards. Resentment at the loss
of these underpaid black serfs further encouraged elaborate
dissertations on black ingratitude and dire prophesies of the
Negro's future as well as the sinister resurgence of the Klan.

The post-war era saw the emergence of the new Negro,
described by Alaine Locke in his preface to *The New
Negro*. It was also the time of the Garvey Movement, the
glorification of blackness, the Negro renaissance in the arts,
the discovery of African primitive arts, the glorification of
the exotic primitive—a whole flowering of activity—artistic,
intellectual, political, social, and educational. In the South
the Negro's popularity as a literary topic resulted in a
number of books sympathetic to the Negro share-cropper
and field-hand. As John Bradbury says, "in 1922, three
novelists from three separate states brought into the open
the Negro's social and economic problems, as plantation
worker, city dweller, and small-town reformer. Before the
end of the decade, Dubose Heyward, Julia Peterkin, Robert
E. Kennedy, Roark Bradford, and others had assumed the
Negro's point of view to explore a variety of conditions and
attitudes in Southern communities." Mr. Bradbury continues, "Though the social views manifested by the authors of
these books with Negro orientation were by no means
uniformly liberal, or even critical of white prejudice, the
curiosity and observation of the authors suggested new
forces at work."[1]

Such authors inclined toward the use of the exotic-primitive stereotype. Vachel Lindsay's poem "The Congo," which points to the primitive, spontaneous, unconventional, and flamboyant qualities of the Negro, became a focal point for this literary fad. His poem, subtitled, "A Study of the Negro Race," was divided into three parts which serve to outline the characteristic ideas of his followers: "Their Basic Savagery," "Their Irrepressible High Spirits," and "The Hope of Their Religion." In the post-war revolt against Puritanism and Babbittry, and in the new enthusiasm for Freudian sexual psychology, artistic expressiveness, and primitive aesthetic values, the 'twenties turned to the "savage inheritance" of the Negro: "hot jungle nights, the tom-tom calling to esoteric orgies."[2] This whole frenzied fad, which was largely centered in Harlem and which provided the basis for the Negro renaissance of the period, Sterling Brown insists, is really rooted in the old Sambo-contented-slave tradition. While Van Vechten's followers wrote about the fast set of gamblers and red-hot mammas, the Southern primitivists found delight in the contentment and charm and quaint views of the inhabitants of Catfish Row, Blue Brook Plantation, and the Mississippi cane-brakes.

Among the best known of these early studies of contemporary Negroes, figuring centrally in the narratives, are Porgy and Bess, Dubose Heyward's star-crossed lovers. Tenants of a recognizable locale, Charleston, they live the primitive life of the Catfish Row residents. Their pleasure is in the sex, music, laughter, picnicking, and narcotics typical of such people. Their need for security, for love, and for excitement are quite believable. Their response to birth, to sickness, to separation, and to death is human enough to distinguish them from the plantation stereotypes.

The later, less primitive, more perceptive study of the

Negro by Heyward, *Mamba's Daughters*, illustrates an even greater effort to understand the life pattern of the modern Negro. The book has little of *Porgy*'s simple charm and flashing color: the characters are less types and somewhat more individualized, but the result is disappointing. Neither a brilliant study of Negro life nor a study-in-depth of Negro psychology, the story is an interesting failure. It does show the shrewdness behind the devoted servant pose, the ability of the Negro to use white people to his own advantage, the aspirations Negro parents cherish for their children, the sacrifices they are willing to make, as well as the confusion the mulatto child feels when forced to become socially superior to her own family. In such a study as this, it is tempting to prefer *Mamba's Daughters* to *Porgy*, but its sincerity and significance make it less artistic than the simpler, more stylized *Porgy*.

Compared with later stories, these early novels about lower class Negro life look quaint and superficial. Although too much space is given to interesting superstitions and Saturday night revels, at least these authors opened the door to sympathetic treatment of lower class Negroes. Porgy and Mamba and April and Candy are real people with real problems of hunger and poverty and pain. Their psychology is not subtle and their economic plight is not central to their tales, but they have more individuality than some of the later black proletarians. They are appealing, their emotions are touching, their problems fundamental— in spite of their setting in romanticized studies of Southern Negro folk ways.

These exotic primitives suffer from being seen as fascinating largely for their departures from white patterns. The emphasis on exoticism keeps the black primitive from being quite realistic or universal. Colorful rather than painful elements are stressed by authors seeking to entertain, not to reform. The authors seem condescending to the modern reader; they resemble indulgent elders delighted at the charming antics of their black children.

Other novels of more rural Southern Negro life are even less artistic. *Candy*, L.M. Alexander's story of an amoral, happy Negro woman living at the end of the plantation era, shows the vestiges of paternalism that continue in evidence long after slavery was abolished. The Negroes are not slaves nor serfs (in the sense of being tied to the land), but they are content to lead a marginal existence, to enjoy primitive pleasures, and to ignore the world outside. More ambitious members of the community migrate to Harlem and send back glowing messages and offers to help others move North. But Candy, with her men and her songs, is too contented to change. Only a handsome young man from Harlem (luring her away with surprisingly honorable intentions) and the sale of the plantation can blast her loose from her shack. She is certainly an old-fashioned Negro, black, happy, full of laughter and sensuality. She has a simple charm, as does her story, that gives her and it the quality of a fairy tale.

Actually, Candy, like the heroes and heroines of Julia Peterkin's fiction, appears designed to appeal to white readers who hunger for stories of childlike Negroes full of natural high spirits without morality or forethought. In a sophisticated age (the 'twenties) these wood-cut characterizations offer a pastoral alternative to urban confusion that has a certain charm to which confirmed sophisticates offer pious lip-service between cabaret visits.

Julia Peterkin wrote more of these local-color novels than her contemporaries, and on the basis of her efforts established a brief reputation as a leading authority on "The Negro." *Scarlet Sister Mary* is much like *Candy*, the study of a woman without any expectation that men will share the burden of her growing family of illegitimate children. She is somewhat more serious than Candy, more disillusioned, more aware that she is considered a fallen woman by the church people who pursue their pleasures more secretly than she. The story is more realistic than *Candy* and more sensitive to the reality of loneliness and trouble.

But the others among Miss Peterkin's stories are not so well told nor have the characters such poignance as the lonely Mary. *Black April* again shows the young girl bearing her illegitimate child while the carefree young Negro runs off to seduce a new girl. But this time, from the opening scene, Miss Peterkin seems far more intent on cataloguing the fascinating superstitions of these childlike primitives than in telling a story of human emotions. Although interesting in the details of Negro life it reveals, the elaborate tale fails to achieve any effective climax or pattern. When April, the hero, puts his crippled feet in a pail of medicine only to have the toes fall off, the reader is grotesquely delighted instead of sympathetically shocked. The enormous Negro could have been the subject of a tragic drama, but becomes instead a pathetic part of the plantation's Lilliputian quarrels and rivalries. The book suffers from a lack of focus and a lack of unifying theme. *Bright Skin* is no better. The career of the "blue gum" Negro who loves the unfeeling "bright skin" mulatto girl has some sensitivity, but it is difficult to excite the reader's sympathy for a man who insists on being a door mat. The exaggerated emphasis on the charms of the lighter skin replaces deeper motivation for action, and again the catalogues of quaint Negro customs renders the book an anthropological study rather than a novel. We are encouraged to laugh at the religion, sex life, morality, superstition, and trickery of the black primitives. They are not Sambos, however, since they are occasionally capable of experiencing real pain and real shame. But for the most part they bear an unfortunate resemblance to the minstrel tradition.

Even such simplistic treatment of folk characters roused the ire of some reactionary Southern critics, who preferred the old stereotypes to the new ones. And Northern critics were duped into curious pronouncements about the breadth and depth of Miss Peterkin's knowledge of The Negro. It is not surprising that Sterling Brown joined other Negro intellectuals in deriding this fascination with Negro folk as primitive *objets d'art* rather than real human beings.

But with all his superficiality, the exotic primitive opened the door to a new interest in Negro characterization. With the Depression, the Negro renaissance and its enthusiasm for Negro art and literature came to an abrupt halt. But the literary characters who had evolved in the 'twenties were to survive their originators. The exotic primitive became the black proletarian in the North and the black cropper in the South; the new Negro became the Negro intellectual and then the civil rights leader.

In the meantime, Negro writers continued to write. In the next era the Federal Writers Project, a part of the W.P.A., employed a number of Negro writers—Richard Wright, Arna Bontemps, William Attaway, Ralph Ellison, Frank Yerby among Southern Negroes—and even published an anthology of Negro writings under the title *American Stuff* (Viking Press, 1937), thereby keeping the Negro's attention focused on the arts. The liberal arts, which had replaced the more expensive manual training programs in many Negro schools in the South as well as in the North, were growing increasingly important to the Negro, and were drawing him away from the Booker T. Washington formula of accommodation and deliberate progress.

But much attention was necessarily expended during the Depression decade on the purely practical problem of survival. The boom of the post-war years had brought enormous numbers of Negroes to the cities, and now these unskilled workers were the first to be laid off. As Robert Bone describes the period and its impact on Negro writers:

Negro intellectuals were even more responsive to the social crisis of the 1930's than were the whites, in direct proportion to the greater suffering of the Negro masses. Traditionally the last to be hired and the first to be fired, the Negro wage worker bore the brunt of the economic blow. Goaded by his knowledge of the black worker's double burden, the Negro intellectual of the 1930's was readily inclined to support the new movements of social protest.

This new militancy, however, in contrast to that of earlier periods, was social rather than racial in emphasis. It was based on the grievances of the Negro masses rather than on those of the rising middle class. In some instances, under the influence of Marxist ideology, it came to embrace the grievances of the white working class as well. During the Depression, for the first time in their history, the Negro masses made common cause with their white fellows in the campaign of organized labor for higher wages, union recognition, and greater unemployment benefits. As a result of their trade-union experience, the Negro masses began to break through the narrow confines of their lives and enter a broader arena of social struggle.[3]

One of the clearest responses of the intellectual and the nonintellectual Negro to the Depression was the shifting of his thinking from racial to class channels. The Negro found white toilers increasingly willing to join him in the campaign for higher wages and union recognition. "During the depression," says Hugh Gloster, "strikers and demonstrators of both races banded together to demand relief and jobs. Even in such states as Arkansas and Mississippi black and white tenants and sharecroppers, kept apart in earlier years by race-baiting demagogues, sometimes collaborated in spite of threats, violence, and accusations of 'Red Russianism.'"[4]

From this point on there has been a flirtation between the Negro and the Communist Party,[5] undoubtedly magnified by Southern racists but mentioned incidentally and clearly several times in novels. Richard Wright was attracted to the Party because it "did not say 'Be like us and we will like you, maybe.' It said: 'If you possess enough courage to speak out what you are, you will find that you are not alone.'"[6] (He also tells of his experience with communism in the more elaborate discussion, *The God That Failed*, 1949.) He, like Ellison, found in Party work the sense of belonging so essential to the alienated Negro intellectual, as well as the ritual and guidance of established institutions so valuable for those whose personalities had been so systematically destroyed by slavery and the post-Civil War dislocations. Bone says of Wright that his contribution to the Negro novel "was precisely his fusion of a pronounced racialism with a broader tradition of social protest,"[7] or turning the Negro novel into the proletarian novel. The scenes of the "Brotherhood" in Ellison's book underline a similar experience: the original temptation to join the "Brotherhood" because of the absence of a color line, the later recognition of the Party's use of the Negro as a whip against the rest of the community, and finally the break with the Party.

There are few explicit references in good novels to this period and mood. Of them, Ellison's "Brotherhood" section in *Invisible Man* is the most perceptive. He shows the young Negro, having migrated North, failing to find permanent work, concerned that his abilities have no outlet. Suddenly, provoked to express the mood of the crowd watching an old Negro couple being dispossessed, he finds himself giving a moving speech against the evils of

capitalism. When the crowd changes into a mob and he is
in danger of being arrested as the instigator of a riot, he
runs. But the alert Brotherhood observers have spotted
him as a potential leader who could prove of use to
them—even though he is not black enough. They find him
difficult to handle, though, since he tends to orate
spontaneously without proper concern for their theories,
he can not adapt quickly to new emphases handed down
from headquarters, he is too personally ambitious, and he
is race-conscious rather than class-conscious. Other Negroes in the Brotherhood are equally obstreperous: Tod
has too much pride, is too emotional and unpredictable;
and Westrum is less concerned with ideology than with
forcing white men to shake his hand.

Ellison appears to feel that the Communists (insofar as
they may be identified with the Brotherhood) failed to
understand the American Negro. They did not realize that
their appeal to the Negro is not based on class and is not
transferable. Unless they are dealing specifically with
Negro problems in America, they will lose most Negro
support. They assume falsely that Negroes are an ideolo-
gically concerned people. But Ellison shows his Harlem
inhabitants as simple, shrewd people who have lived with
treachery for years, and who know when they are being
used or being double-crossed. No ideological double-talk
clouds their judgment. When the Brotherhood abandons
those projects designed to arouse Harlem to concern for its
economic plight, then it loses its Harlem membership. The
Negro, long a tool of the white man, is suspicious of the
proffered friendship of any white organization.

The invisible man himself is not fully dedicated to the
Brotherhood from the time he hears Jack tell him that the
old dispossessed couple are not important—they are rural
people in our industrial society, the victims of history. He

knows that human anguish matters, history or no history. When later the Brotherhood turns its back on the problems of the Negro because of a new committee decision, the Negro hero cannot move with the organization. He has seen too much of slavery to sacrifice his decisions to committee verdict. He is tired of having white people tell him what to do, what to think, and what to be. He refuses to be ordered or defined by anyone other than himself. Calling Brother Jack, "Marse Jack," he emphasizes that this surrender to the tyranny of the Brotherhood would be a virtual return to slavery—a "boomerang" of history. Leaving the Brotherhood proves traumatic. For a time he had believed in it: "it was the only historically meaningful life that I could live. If I left it, I'd be nowhere. As dead and as meaningless as Clifton." But he decides to opt for individualism, to make the "plunge outside of history."

Ellison explains his hero's disillusionment: "They had set themselves up to describe the world. What did they know of us, except that we numbered so many, worked on certain jobs, offered so many votes, and provided so many marchers for some protest parade of theirs?" And he says, a little later, "Here I had thought they accepted me because they felt that color made no difference, when in reality it made no difference because they didn't see color or men . . . . For all they were concerned, we were so many names scribbled on fake ballots, to be used at their convenience and when not needed to be filed away." To everyone, even to the "Brotherhood," the Negro hero is still nothing—an invisible man.

Another example of the Negro Marxist is far more individualistic than Ellison's. After all, Ellison in *Invisible Man* is striving to explain his own career in typical terms, to make of himself a symbol of the Negro people. His Negro Communists must perforce be types; the black prince (Tod Clifton), the ex-convict (Tarp), the leveler (Westrum), and the semi-dedicated opportunist (the hero). But Carson McCullers had no such central purpose in writing *The Heart Is a Lonely Hunter*. As her title indicates, she is concerned with those people who for various reasons are cut off from the mainstream of life. The Communist in the South is such a person, less interesting to Miss McCullers for his politics than for his isolation.

The Negro doctor in the story finds that his education separates him from most of his race and even his family. It ruins his marriage and even alienates his children, who cannot understand his desire to better himself and improve them. In the face of their impenetrable ignorance, he appears hysterical with frustration. In communism, which he accepts as a logical explanation for the problems he sees around him, he finds a comfort but he cannot respond to the white activist Communist who comes to argue with him. Dr. Copeland's gentle Marxism has none of the anger and need for revolution seen among more violent members of the persuasion. When his annual award for an essay by an exceptional Negro youth goes to a young Communist full of black power aggressions, the gentle old doctor is saddened. The frantic but brilliant young Negro essayist turns his sexual and psychological disturbances into the channels of race hatred. His ambition, he says, is to be like those Communist attorneys who defended the Scottsboro boys. The committment of this fine mind to revenge and anger pains the doctor, who has given his life to healing and gradual reform. His own career seems to him to have been wasted, and now the next generation will not even accept his pacific program for social reform. In Carson McCuller's novel, the communism is no more important than it is in Faulkner's later works. Linda Snopes is a Communist, but this is no threat to Yoknapatowpha

County. It is only another evidence, like her deafness and her strange speech, of her difference from her people and her neighbors. Dr. Copeland too is one of those numerous studies of the lonely, misunderstood Southerner.

Miss McCullers' mention of the Scottsboro case is echoed in *Native Son*, when Bigger Thomas is also defended by Communist attorneys interested in making him a tool for their political propaganda. Richard Wright, writing out of his own experience with the Party, points to this opportunism of the Communists, noting that Negroes involved in labor troubles are often tempted to join with the Communists because they offer black laborers aid at propitious moments. It has been a typical accusation by the extremists that any labor agitation or Negro unrest in the South is Communist-inspired (a judgment frequently expressed by the racist white characters in Negro-centered fiction), but actually the only incitement that Negro workers may need is the simple awareness of being so thoroughly and systematically exploited. Both *Strange Fruit* and *The Little Foxes*, Lillian Hellman's frightening play about the voracious new industrialists of the South, comment on the blatant exploitation of Southern labor.

Apparently this phase of Southern Negro-oriented fiction was a brief movement growing out of the liberal, sympathetic fiction of the 'twenties. In the Depression 'thirties and early 'forties, "radical and militantly liberal" fiction began to appear in the South. "In stories centered on Negroes and poor whites, as well as in novels of industrial strife," says John Bradbury, "a substantial number of Southerners joined the national trend, enlisting their full sympathies with the exploited, the uprooted, the deprived. Faced by avowed radicals of the industrial scene, like Myra Page, Grace Lumpkin, Leane Zugsmith, and Olive Durgan, and reinforced by staunch liberals adopting Negro and red-neck points of view, this group attacked the traditional prejudices and hypocrisies which an economic collapse had exposed."[8]

These Depression years made the Negro novel America's most popular proletarian novel form, containing the prominent virtues and vices of that form: although often emotionally moving and socially valuable, such novels tempt readers to judge them by the accuracy of their observations and the power of their protest rather than by their artistry or poetic insight. Seen from a distance in time, they often seem hackneyed and confined to the era which they strove to reform. Seldom do they rise to the more universal heights of a *Grapes of Wrath* or a *Golden Boy*, other products of the same era and the same kind of moral prodding.

As for the other novels that deal with union activity in the South, most are not of remarkably high caliber. Richard Wright pictures a few strike scenes in his short story collection *Uncle Tom's Children*, disclosing that the Negro remained the favorite scapegoat for brutal whites. White men whip one Negro leader and kill another as punishment for union activities. His *12 Million Black Voices* is a more prosaic and forthright commentary on the Negroes during this same period. Ted Poston's "The Making of Mamma Harris" (in *The Negro Caravan*) is the sketch of a mammy type metamorphosized into a union leader in a tobacco factory. Waters Turpin shows some strike scenes in his novel of the Negroes in Chicago during the Depression years, *O Canaan!* He notes that unions which had not wanted or needed Negro members before, now both needed and wanted them.

Among the few really successful Southern narratives of the Negro involved in union strife is William Attaway's *Blood on the Forge*. Attaway describes a family of Southern Negroes who grow weary of their hand-to-mouth existence on the farm and succumb to the blandishments of a scout for Northern industry who offers the three men transportation to Pittsburgh and work in a steel mill. The men represent three Negro types: Big Mat is the religious family-man; Chinatown is the pagan, irresponsible Sambo; Melody is the sympathetic, thoughtful, sensitive poet. Leaving their family behind, they emigrate hoping for success and immediate reunion in the Northern paradise. They find however that factory work is more demanding and less rewarding than they had suspected, that the white workers are hostile toward them, and that their discouragement and weariness render them susceptible to the enticements of the big city. The book becomes a poignant chronicle of their disintegration. Melody gives up his guitar; Mat abandons his Bible and his dreams of being reunited with his wife; and Chinatown stops his happy laughter. As they abandon their habits and memories, they try to find new interests in the city. But women, liquor, and fights leave them literally castrated and blinded. Ellison believes that Attaway effectively portrays in this story the "destruction of the folk but missed its rebirth on a higher level."

At the time, any rebirth must have seemed dubious at best. Industrial life is apparently no panacea for Attaway's heroes, nor does the union offer brotherhood for these brutalized victims of the industrial revolution. The mutual suspicion among the national and racial groups at the mills is aggravated by the owners' use of Negroes as spies and strikebreakers. The early rejection by the union has made them outsiders, unable to sense their common interests with the laboring group. In a patently false conclusion, the now-enlightened Negroes appear on the brink of a rapprochement with their laboring white brothers in the benevolent bosom of the union. But nothing else in the tone of this otherwise starkly tragic story suggests this as a legitimate conclusion to the tangled lives of the Negroes involved.

This forced conclusion is parallel to the propagandistic novel by Myra Page, *Gathering Storm*, another union-centered story of the 'thirties, which is a veritable parody of proletarian fiction. In contains, for example, such chapter headings as: "Solidarity Forever," "Class against Class," and "In Union there is Strength," in addition to this melodramatic finale: "Our generation's born to struggle. But the stakes, comrades—the stakes come high."

Although the mood of union activity was to bring the warring races together to revamp as warring classes, Attaway realized, like other authors of the time, that Negroes often found difficulty in seeing beyond their Southern background. Having had no experience in the new battle lines drawn by the unions, they tended to believe that color must remain the basis of any dispute. Attaway aimed at discrediting Negro nationalism and promoting class consciousness. McCullers' Dr. Copeland expresses much the same idea: "The injustice of need must bring us all together and not separate us. We must remember that we all make things on this earth of value because of our labor."

Edward Kimbrough's *Night Fire* shows more precisely the precarious balance needed to keep white and black workers satisfied with one another. In this story, the author tells of the years when the bosses used Negro scabs to whip poor whites into accepting abysmal working and living conditions. One astute leader finally shows the workers that, by uniting labor against capital instead of white against black, they can run their own business and be no man's slave. But in spite of their eventual prosperity resulting from this common effort, at any moment, with almost any provocation, the race war may resume.

The real need in the 'thirties was for a black man's *Grapes of Wrath*. Attaway's novel comes as close as any to serving that need, reflecting as it does something of the nature of the great migration taking place. The combination of the Depression and the boll weevil proved too much for the South. Land owners had to tell croppers who had lived all their lives on the land, and whose parents had lived on the same land, that this year there would be no crop. The Negroes were pushed off the land, and jobs in Southern industry were not open to them. Not only were they barred from the textile mills, but even from their traditional occupations as barbers and waiters, carpenters, masons, painters, and saw-mill operators. The onslaught of the Depression forced whites into these jobs and left the Negro penniless, homeless, and unemployed. Thus the North, for all its terrors of climate and foreignness loomed as the only hope. A new migration came, not like the hopeful 'twenties when 800,000 Negroes left the former Confederacy. The 400,000 who left in the 'thirties were not the aggressive new Negroes. They were the submissive, industrious accommodating Uncle Toms. Tenants long accustomed to the Southern paternalistic system suddenly had to fend for themselves, to develop more initiative and self-reliance than ever before.

The era marked the end of the old paternalism, the end of close ties between Negro and white families, the end of the loyal family retainer. The New Deal and social security made the Negro turn from his white folks to his government for his hand-outs, and paradoxically, something both condescending and evil, both warm and compassionate and cruel and enervating went out of the Old South.[9] As Clark explains the change:

Southern racial paternalism was largely destroyed. Only the lumber and pulpwood industries have maintained so close a control over laborers as the farm. Away from the farm the southern Negro has to live off his wages, earned in many instances in the employ of an impersonal corporation or company which supplies no "furnish" and has no other casual credit system. The breaking down of the old easy-going but ruinous relationships of the southern farm has come close to making meaningless cliches of much of what the southern white man thought and said about the Negro.[10]

In this change we see the seeds for the destruction not only of mammy and Uncle Tom, but Sambo and the exotic primitive and the black Ulysses as well—all products of the old, "ruinous" system of Southern rural economy.

Strangely enough, as the share-cropping system was disintegrating, it became an increasingly popular literary topic. The new stories that emerged pictured the cropper not as an exotic primitive but as an economic victim. Authors pointed out the specific evils of the share-cropping system, which often held Negroes in virtual peonage. In 1937, George E. Lee wrote *River George* largely to show the abuses of this system as they would appear to an educated Negro. Lee's bright young hero cannot challenge a crooked bookkeeper, cannot enjoy the fruits of his labor, and cannot even hope to be safe from personal harm. More vicious still are Erskine Caldwell's short stories that picture the horrors of the system. His "Kneel to the Rising Sun" is a graphic study in the sadism of the red-neck boss and the sniveling sycophancy of the poor-white croppers. The Negro shows sympathy with the victims and outspoken disgust at the inhumanity of the boss. The outspoken criticism brings him nothing but violent death. No problems are solved and no hearts changed. "Saturday Afternoon," recounts the murder of an aspiring Negro farmer, as do numerous other of Caldwell's better stories. Ralph McGill speaks of the "cold-eyed, cruel, calculated rapacious exploitation" of the Negro under the old system of Southern paternalism, but these authors dramatize this evil so that it lives in our mind's eye as the bare statement can never do. We can see for a long time afterwards the old white man in Caldwell's story crawling in to share the pigs' food, only to be killed and eaten by those pigs—there is no more graphic way of explaining that these people were being slowly and systematically starved.

During this period the hard-working share-cropper became an increasingly popular literary subject, often treated with great sympathy by Southern artists. One book stands out as less propagandistic and more gentle than the others of this group. Jefferson Young's *A Good Man* is a tranquil study of a cropper's dream—roots in the community, a family to love, and a white house to live in. He stands in the midst of a transitional period, with some whites recognizing the value of a good man (his landlord supports his efforts to improve his weather-beaten old shack by painting it white), while others still live in the bygone era of the booming sawmill and the hordes of subservient Negro laborers. Although the store owner cuts off Albert's furnish and incites local whites to terrorize him, the farmer who owns Albert's house realizes that men like this must be treated better if the Southern economy is to have any future. The South can no longer afford the luxury of prejudice and tyranny.

A number of others writing about the share-cropper's lot have chosen a somewhat more materialistic emphasis. *Inchin' Along* is the story of Dink Britt, a Negro farmer in Alabama who becomes a kind of faithful Griselda type—suffering silently and stoically through the abuses of white neighbors, the seduction and blinding of his wife, the tarring, feathering, and accidental burning of his best friend, and his own near lynching. But he keeps "inchin' along" collecting money, land, and eventually the respect of the community. With his quiet acceptance of every sadistic torment that his community chooses to hand out, his eternal and seemingly sincere obsequiousness, and his single-minded quest for wealth, he is completely unbelievable. Although the story is clearly intended to portray the triumph of this simple but wily man, Dink is too much of an embryonic black Babbitt to be as satisfying as the more human and more idealistic Albert of Jefferson Young's book.

Amber Satyr is a less serious effort at the hard-working tenant-farmer portrayal and is involved more sensationally with problems of miscegenation. Luther, the hero, discovers "that being poor and being a Negro carry their own penalties"—among which are the fear of white men visiting his attractive wife, the peril of a lascivious white woman's insistence on leaping into his bed, and the problem of a half-white daughter's habit of bedding down with any white trash available.

Free Born, by contrast, is a determined effort to make a complete catalogue of the wrongs suffered by the exploited Negro. The bitterness and the incredible endurance of the hero make it more of a tract than a novel. *Georgia Nigger* also emphasizes the horrors of peonage in addition to those of the convict labor system and the chain gang. The hero, David Jackson, discovers that his life becomes a choice between these two hells. *High John the Conqueror* emphasizes the sexual threat as well as the drive to become a landowner. This story pictures the last days of sharecropping in the area and the advent of the large, new, mechanized farms.

A short story by Andrew Nelson Lytle called "Runagate Niggers" is an especially effective and remarkably artistic miniature of this Southern peonage system. The white narrators are more sympathetic to dogs than they are to the Negroes who are controlled by ruthless bosses and corrupt lawmen. When an observer tips off the Federal Government and causes the offending whites to be arrested on a peonage charge, the white commentators are outraged: "Things have come to a pretty pass when a man can't catch his own runagate niggers!"[1] [1]

The black cropper is the most successful of the Southern attempts to picture the black proletarian, since he is more characteristic of the South than the black Communist or the black union-member or the black factory-worker. He clearly differs from the earlier exotic primitive in the greater travail of his life, the greater anguish he must survive, the greater strenuousness of his efforts—in short in the greater seriousness with which he is pictured. The new authors chose to see the victimization rather than the exoticism of the Negro farmer. Interest in the romantic primitive was temporarily replaced by the wrath of the naturalistic reformer. But this was a short-lived stereotype, a part of the mass-hero fad of the 'thirties. In none of his appearances was he very interesting or artistic. His dreams were largely economic and his life was uniformly painful. His triumphs could therefore seldom be more than a pitiful accumulation of land and wealth—poor stuff out of which to create great literature. A product of the Depression mentality, his popularity declined with reviving prosperity.

Harper Lee's *To Kill a Mockingbird* contains one of the few post-war portraits of the poor, hard-working young Negro. Like the earlier studies, he is attractive, concerned with his family, polite, and intelligent. Like them, he is victimized by poor whites and corrupt law. But the tone is different and the portrait is different from the earlier proletarian novels. We now feel that the community is ashamed of its role, that the poor-white Ewells will be punished for their tyranny over the Negroes, that Tom Robinson need not always be a victim to brutal whites and one-sided law. He is a real person, not simply a stereotyped economic victim. His death produces great anguish because the reader has come to appreciate this decent, gentle man. Symbolically Tom is useful as an example of the foolish waste and useless pain resulting from man's blind hate and injustice. Harper Lee sees the possibility of change, symbolized by the fact that she focuses the novel on the lawyer (representing determination to evolve a better system) rather than the Negro victim, and tells it in the words of a child (representing the hope for a less prejudice-bound future) who pities the Negro and loves him. Such a story cannot be classed with the naturalistic narratives of the 'thirties. Tom is more of a person; he is capable of understanding his plight, of fighting for justice, and of despairing when disappointed.

Actually Erskine Caldwell's numerous stories about industrious but abused Negro share-croppers are the most effective of all the anti-peonage efforts. His cruel, barren style is perfect for the portrayal of the intelligent and industrious young Negroes trying to pull themselves and their families out of the mire, hated and dreaded by trashy white tenants, and eventually destroyed by the system and its unthinking and sadistic members. His stories usually end in a lynching or at least a destruction of the man's hopes and his efforts at the hands of sinister *Tobacco Road* types.

One of the few successors of this black worker of the 'thirties is the black businessman. He is industrious, intelligent, concerned with his family, moral, and ambitious—a middle-class Dink Britt (or industrious drudge).

John Ehle shows him building up a taxi business, and Waters Turpin shows him as a storekeeper, restaurateur, etc. Turpin has tried to picture Booker T. Washington's ideal Negro: industrious, polite, clever, investing in his own business, hiring his own people, growing rich, but never too proud to work with his hands. Zora Neale Hurston, who also pictures this black Horatio Alger on occasion, has the intelligence to challenge the bourgeois ideal. In her white-centered novel (*Seraph on the Suwanee*) and her black-centered one (*Their Eyes Were Watching God*) she pictures the rise of the bourgeoisie and explores the validity of the materialistic dream. *Their Eyes Were Watching God* is an especially effective attack on black Babbittry. This remarkable novel is the chronicle of Janie, an attractive and sensitive Negro girl who marries once for security and finds sterility, once for affection and wins social position, and finally for adventurous love and finds heartbreak and partial fulfillment. Her soul needs freedom and experience, not security and power and wealth. But significantly, her search for real values comes after the acquisition of material wealth proves unsatisfying. This cannot become a paradigm for Negro-centered novels until more Negroes have known and reject affluence. To the Dink Britt type of dirt farmer, money is the closest thing to heaven.

Most of the modern novels show the Negro leaving the land to find his success or his tragedy in the city. Times have changed since the day that Stribling's Colonel Vaiden was surprised to discover that a Negro might desire any life outside of personal service to white people or when Wright saw no jobs open to a Negro outside of portering and servile labor. The Negro, forced from the land and from paternalism, has found himself in cities, often in Northern cities, away from his family, from his religion, from his old forms of labor, and from his traditional areas of security.

The Negro industrial worker is rare in Southern fiction, although he is a common part of Northern urban literature. When he appears, it is most often as a character who has evolved from the tale of the displaced cropper. Ellison, Wright, and Attaway have written classic parables of the metamorphosis of the Southern folk Negro into the Northern urban Negro. With the emigration from the Southern states, such pilgrimages were inevitable material for literature—especially since the authors themselves usually emigrated North with the folk. The black innocent, driven from his home and family, dreaming of a Northern utopia, becomes the rootless victim of the depersonalized, industrialized North. In such a parable, the Negro serves as innocence corrupted by experience, agrarian virtues destroyed by urban vices, and dreams exploded by reality. These are archetypal patterns of individual and collective human change, transcending the purely economic definition of man and his world.

Clearly the 'thirties marked a change in the image of the Negro. The Southerner sees him more often as an economic and social victim, not simply as an interesting folk type. Fired from industry like white men, or driven off the land like white men, Negroes began to look like depressed humans, not members of a peculiar alien species. Sympathy was bound to develop as problems were clearly shared problems, not exclusively racial ones.

Pictures of depressed conditions are now out-of-fashion. Only a James Agee or a Richard Wright can still interest the modern audience in the plight of the Southern rural Negro. In an affluent age, the victim of economics, no matter how innocent and hard-working, makes dreary fiction. The black 'cropper, for all his touted virtues, is usually wooden and uninspired. We sympathize with his plight, pity his anguish, applaud his rise, but grow weary of his personality. He is the typical mass-hero—significant but uninteresting, better sociology than art.

8

THE NEW SOUTHERN NEGRO

The Negro character unanimously judged the most likely to be lynched is the new Negro, who was new to the North after World War I, but has appeared in conspicuous numbers in the South only since World War II. When a flashy, cynical Negro wandered through Southern "nigger-town" in a novel of the 'thirties, we knew that Sportin' Life was a "Harlem nigger," one that bred admiration and temptation in his Southern brethren. But contact with him was clearly disastrous. Porgy's Bess immediately began to take "happy dust" because of his serpentine wheedling, and ended up debased and jailed. Everyone on Catfish Row knew that a Harlem Negro in Charleston could mean nothing but trouble.

Other novels of the 'twenties and 'thirties record the rare visits of these emissaries of the Northern utopias as if they were dropped down from another planet. When Mrs. Alexander's Candy sees such people, she first rejects them as a threat to her traditional way of life on the plantation and then succumbs to one especially sweet-talking, but decent city slicker. Northern emancipated Negroes upset the primitive life of Miss Peterkin's Negroes too. In *Bright Skin*, one of the local boys goes off to become a famous preacher in Harlem, and other members of the community gradually join him, to the head-shaking concern of the older and more conservative Negroes.

The exotic flavor of such visits and the vivid contrast of these characters with the traditional Southern rural Negro stereotypes underline the alien quality of the new Negro, who was portrayed largely as a free-living, free-thinking, free-loving Harlem Sportin' Life until he began to invade the South in numbers large enough to invite more careful consideration. This character has finally become the diametric opposite of the faithful servant type. It is as if Br'er Rabbit had suddenly become Br'er Fox. While the mammy is old, loyal, and ignorant, the new Negro is generally young, independent, and educated. Because he has matured in a literary period when derogatory stereotypes are in disfavor, he is more likely to appear as either a compensatory stereotype, as an individual, or simply as a type.

He may assume various roles: the happy-go-lucky but shrewd Negro, the aggressive agitator for civil rights, the professional man, or the community leader—any of which may partake of the more urbane, enlightened, independent spirit. In almost all of these cases, the character has more education than earlier Negro characters who were victims of the deficient, segregated Southern educational system that made the illiterate primitive a part of life as well as of local-color literature.

In spite of the pre-Civil War laws forbidding Negro education, there have always been some educated Negroes in the South. One critic has traced the historical origins of this middle-class educated Negro to

the nocturnal escapades of countless male aristocrats who tried valiantly to wash a whole race whiter than snow. When "Massa" had an illegitimate child by a Negro slavewoman, his attitude toward his offspring was often ambivalent. On the one hand, he desired a better destiny for his child than the cotton patch and the overseer's lash. On the other hand, manumission was often legally impossible, and in any case it constituted too public an acknowledgement. Above all, it created a free colored population whose very existence threatened the institution of slavery.

Eventually a compromise was effected, by creating a privileged group of mulatto house servants who were relieved of the more arduous duties of the darker field hands. A division of labor resulted, roughly corresponding to complexion, and soon hardened along class lines. The house servants, living in greater proximity to their white masters, enjoyed freer access to the dominant culture. Notwithstanding the letter of the law, they often learned to read and write, and in some cases even assisted with the administration of the plantation.[1]

Elizabeth Coker's *Daughter of Strangers* is a detailed study of a light-colored girl who is taken into the house and educated, eventually taking over much of the administration of the plantation. Her lot is in stark contrast with that of the darker, illiterate field-hands. Nat Turner, a darker Negro house servant, joins his mother in sneering at the field "niggers" who have fewer advantages than those who live in the big house. His mother, a cook, is shocked at being forced to use a privy with such common folk, asserting that she and her son are "quality." Nat, accepting his mother's snobbery, grows increasingly isolated from his childhood playmates, whose Negro dialect becomes incomprehensible to his ears, whose limited vocabulary stirs scorn in his heart, and whose circumscribed way of life is so alien to his own experience. Unlike the other Negroes on the Turner plantation, Nat learns to read and write. He can figure as far as algebra, and he has memorized much of the Bible. But Styron, in an interesting study of slave psychology, suggests that the education and the hope for manumission are the very reasons for Nat's later violent rebellion.

Nat and the creamy-complexioned house servants were so unlike most of the field Negroes that they were not a popular subject for white writers of fiction for many years. Not only were they not "typical" Negroes, they also focused on unfortunate implications: the illicit origin of the mulattoes, the reason for the educational advantages of the middle-class (or the "Talented Tenth"), and the possibility that the Negro was more than a quaint creature with a child's brain. When the educated Negro appeared in white fiction, his intelligence was attributed to his white blood (the tragic mulatto cliche). Thus, a dark Negro scholar, like Nat Turner or those in W.E.B. Dubois' novels, are exceptions to the fictional pattern. Styron was not even tempted to succumb to cliches since he was dealing with an historical character whose blackness was a source of his pride.

Some of the more recent novelists comment on the inadequate Negro educational system, especially in the nineteenth century. Both Elizabeth Coker and T.S. Stribling criticize the ante-bellum laws forbidding the education of Negroes, and both show free-thinking white slave-owners flouting the law and giving lessons to their pet slaves. But they admit that the mulatto house servants rather than the black field hands usually profited by such teaching. Styron's study of the slave rebel is a rare example of a novel explaining the very real reasons for keeping the slaves ignorant.

On the other hand, early Negro writers, such as W.W. Brown, Frank J. Webb, Martin Delany, and Mrs. E.W. Harper, using their novels as propaganda tools, did picture educated Negroes: "Decorous, educated, aspiring heroes who surmount the stumbling blocks of race to become successful politicians, lawyers, teachers, journalists, ministers, and physicians."[2] While white novelists were ignoring this rising middle-class, Negro novelists at the turn of the century emphasized their role in an effort to counteract the propaganda of negrophobe white novelists. After all, it was in the best interests of the white community to assume that slavery was a benevolent system and that freemen were uniformly miserable or criminal. The discontented freeman is a natural corollary to the stereotype of the contented slave. Thus, while Thomas Dixon and Thomas Nelson Page continued their slave propaganda, Negro novelists undertook counter-propaganda. Such authors, writing before World War I, usually portrayed

educated and well-mannered colored characters, frequently related by blood to the Southern aristocracy, who often engage in long discussions of racial and political issues and are almost invariably presented as teachers, clergymen, physicians, lawyers, politicians, or journalists. The favorite practice is the depiction of these individuals attending lectures, literary societies, political councils, and institutions of higher education. In order to emphasize the plight of their race, Negro authors described such mistreatment as insult, malicious propaganda, Jim-Crowism, legal injustice, economic exploitation, illicit sexual relationships, peonage, lynching, and rioting, which often bring misery and tragedy not only to Negroes but to whites as well.[3]

Such fiction has spawned the problem novels, the proletarian novels, the civil-rights novels of more recent years. They have been, for the most part, abnormal growths in the South, where the scarcity of educated Negroes has been painfully apparent.

Not only have opportunities for a good education been scarce, but the rewards for the educated man have been paltry. White writers and white citizens long after emancipation argued against improvements in Negro education. Negroes were unready for education, they insisted; Negroes furthermore did not need schooling for their hewing of wood, etc. Learning would only make them dissatisfied with their lot (a lot which was clearly ordained by a just, white God); consequently education would make them candidates for insurrection. The arguments have not really changed much over the years. The Negroes themselves, for a long while, saw little reason for learning, since it was so poorly rewarded. Miss Peterkin's people (in the 'twenties and 'thirties) are uneducated and see no need to change; they consider it unlucky to tamper with books. Spoken words are safer, the exotic primitives say in *Scarlet Sister Mary*. One cook, this time in *Black April*, does see the possible value in being able to read recipes, but on the other hand Miss Peterkin points out that she is a superlative cook without book learning. And her daughter, who does go to school, returns to the same primitive life of the farm instead of using her education to escape; so her education is largely wasted.

Stribling, in a less sentimental and condescending way, says that owners prefer share-croppers who cannot read or cipher: such Negroes question fewer of the bills and are by and large more pliable. His white characters, both aristocrats and poor whites, generally resent educated Negroes. One of the most painful scenes in Stribling's novels is the burning of the Negro schoolhouse (in *The Store*) by resentful and ignorant white croppers. Even the more modern stories continue to reflect the resentment against educating Negroes. In Lonnie Colemen's *Clara*, the narrator, Lillian, asserts that Negroes do not need much education; that is why their schools have fewer grades. She assumes that her own white nephew will go on to college, but her husband's equally bright mulatto son is expected to leave school and become a farmer. Even as a farmer, he arouses resentment because he reads farm journals and experiments in improving farming methods. (He is murdered by a white man because of his refusal to play the obsequious role that society has ordained for him—a parallel to a similar situation with the bright young mulatto farmer in Stribling's earlier novel *The Store*.)

Many Southern whites have been delighted at the popularity of Booker T. Washington's emphasis on manual labor. A large number of Negroes have also seen his program as at least an interim solution by which they may insure Negro prosperity and the gradual acclimation of Southern whites to Negro education. Waters Turpin, for example, is a Negro novelist who (in *O Canaan!*) champions much of Washington's platform. He shows the prosperous Negro (significantly, having gone North for the opportunity to profit from his skills) who works with his hands or with his brain, whichever is more immediately profitable. The predominant tone, however, in more recent literature, has been toward an acceptance of W.E.B. Dubois' emphasis on the more aggressive pattern of behavior rather than the placatory Washington paradigm. Stribling has two of his educated Negro characters debate the Washington-DuBois controversy and demonstrates in his own story (*Birthright*) that Southern whites are not really willing to allow any progress even by Washington's pacific program.

DuBois was among those early Negro novelists who presented educated Negro characters. He championed the liberal education as opposed to Washington's practical training. DuBois, himself a scholar and a poet, saw no reason that a Negro must conform to the stereotypes white man imposed upon him. A Negro has every right to be an intellectual, whose free play of imagination is not tied to specific needs and practical affairs. But it was only when manual arts proved too expensive that Southerners allowed Negroes to switch to a liberal education.

Thomas Clark comments that this new liberal education in the South was responsible for much of the breaking up of traditional patterns, turning Negroes to fields other than manual labor. "In this area," Clark says of the Negro, "he has made a creditable showing, and it is in this area that over the last twenty years he has come to study subject matter which has had a profound bearing upon his attitudes toward his present position in American democracy. Likewise, this fact has enabled leaders of his own race to mobilize Negro opinion more effectively than ever before in American history."[4]

Traditionally, when an educated Negro has appeared in literature, he has been a philanthropist, seeking to help his people with his knowledge. Even DuBois found it hard to divorce education from practical application. The standard picture of the educated Negro shows him to be the son of a slave and a landed aristocrat, raised by a black mother who supports him by her Herculean efforts, sends him North to college, where he has to work to pay part of his tuition, while she hopes for and dreads his eventual return home. After becoming a doctor, a lawyer, or a teacher, he does return South, marries another liberated black intellectual, and has a family, becoming a respected leader in the black community, keeping up a friendly and humble relationship with local whites. It is the pattern of Booker T. Washington himself and is considered by many modern Negroes the design for Uncle Tomism.

T.S. Stribling, in *Birthright*, varies the classic pattern by accentuating the enormous sacrifice made by Peter Siner, a mulatto teacher who elects to return South; Stribling further shows the irony of the half-hearted welcome home he receives, his disappointment in his efforts to help his people, and his eventual decision to abandon his dream of building a Negro academy. He does marry a bright Negro girl, but she is pregnant by her white employer at the time of their wedding and is despised by the whole black community. Stribling's Negro Harvard-graduate predictably finds that the prejudices and the Jim-Crowism of the community grate on his sensibilities more after his sojourn in the North. And he therefore takes his bride and leaves.

Hamilton Basso's *Courthouse Square* contains parallel distresses for the mulatto doctor who discreetly pretends he is a druggist while trying to win the confidence of the community. When he attempts to buy the empty home of his white father to use for a Negro hospital, he is thwarted by irate white citizens who kill three Negroes and burn the old mansion as well as most of niggertown. Shocked and discouraged, he too abandons hope of bringing progress to benighted Southern Negroes.

The Negro medical man has been especially popular as a literary subject in the last forty years, largely because he is often the only educated Negro in a Southern community. Walter White, in "A Negro Doctor in the South, " shows some of the professional problems a Negro has struggled against: his own people respect a white quack more than they do a competent Negro doctor; he cannot argue with a faulty diagnosis by a white doctor; and no white doctor will assist him in an operation. Barbara Anderson, in *Southbound*, adds to the list as she portrays her Negro doctor in his missionary role in the South: a Negro doctor may not take his patients to a white hospital, and he will find that Negro hospitals, where available, are poorly equipped; a Negro physician may not even sit down in a white doctor's waiting room; nor may he belong to the medical association, where he might express his complaints or learn more about his work. (Some of these problems have been alleviated in recent years.)

For many of their frustrations, Negro doctors, at least in fiction, blame their own people as well as the whites. McCullers' Dr. Copeland tries to teach the impoverished

Negroes in his community about birth control, exhorting them to limit their families. He becomes the first doctor in town to distribute contraceptive devices, but the Negroes continue to breed in poverty and ignorance regardless of his efforts. When he listens to tales of their unmitigated stupidity, he moans, "The Negro race of its own accord climbs up on the cross every Friday." He goes on to explain that they will give all of their money and brains and courage to something silly, but not dedicate themselves to their race or to their own success.

Poor Dr. Copeland cannot convince even his own children to listen to his voice crying out in the wilderness. His heart is the loneliest hunter in the book. In this portrait, Miss McCullers has hit upon a reality for the educated Negro. Stribling too has pointed out such a man's loneliness among his own people; he is cut off completely from the educated white community as well, so that one does not know that the other exists. In Nat Turner's thirty or more years of life, he has only two real friends, and both of them are illiterate. His solitude gives him time to think, to grow bitter, to see visions, and to become the confused and fanatic man he finally develops into. Styron uses Nat's loneliness and his celibacy to explain his violent emotionalism. In *Birthright*, the loneliness of the town's two educated Negroes draws them together; then, finding that they cannot alter their community, they decide to save themselves. This is the ultimate temptation: weary of battle against ignorance and filth, sick of the attitudes of both whites and blacks, the intellectual is tempted to abandon his home and create a life for himself outside of the South. McCullers points out the isolation an unacknowledged prophet feels in his own country and the pain and fury in his heart when he sacrifices his life for his people and they ignore or reject that sacrifice. Paul Green's

Abraham (in *Abraham's Bosom*) is also a lonely hunter, but he at least has a loving wife. Yet he, like Dr. Copeland, finds that his son defies his dream. This is the typical adolescent response to the anguish of watching his parents' misery. The burden of the parent's dream becomes too much for the child to bear, so the child may elect to return to the primitive life that the parent has been striving to escape.

If the Negro characters become lawyers, they seldom return South. Clement Wood's *Nigger* pictures the usual difficulties for the Southern Negro lawyer—poverty, the long struggle to find clients, rejection by Negroes as well as whites, the antagonism of white judges and juries. Couch has noted the problem of a Negro lawyer in the South quite graphically:

Suppose, for instance, that an intelligent young Negro does go to Harvard or Chicago for his advanced training and returns South with, say, a degree in medicine or law. He may easily pass the state examination and be allowed to practice his profession, but his practice will be exclusively limited to Negroes and even among Negroes will be limited to certain types of cases. Judges are invariably white. Juries only rarely will have Negroes on them. Negro offenders often avoid Negro advocates, and Negro lawyers must be extremely careful how they appear before white juries. Even in those counties, towns and cities in which Negroes form the great majority of the population the local government will be entirely in the hands of white people, and the representatives of the state and the federal congress will be white. The Negro is supposed to have the legal right to representation. Actually he does not.[5]

Dubose Heyward shows the condescending attitude toward a Negro lawyer in Charleston by his white associates, who tolerate him only because he acts out the Sambo role. Nor does he know anything of law—witness his home-made divorce forms that have proven such a profitable venture for him. The comment in *Mamba's Daughters* echoes that idea in *Porgy*—here too, the Negro attorney is not a respected part of the judicial structure. The accused Negro receives a stiffer fine for having hired any lawyer at all, and especially a Negro lawyer. More recent Negro lawyers, however, appearing in such novels as *The Southerner* and *The White Band* are no Sambos. They are literate, self-confident, attractive, shrewd, cynical, aggressive, and in every way typical of a new generation of educated Negro characters. They are not afraid of judges; they instigate daring litigation; they know their law, and they constantly risk being lynched by frustrated and puzzled whites whose definition of "nigger" does not include these men.

While lawyers, until recently, have not been inclined to return South, schoolteachers and preachers usually do feel a call to return, but they are often portrayed as barely literate. The preachers were gradually to metamorphosize into aggressive race leaders, but the earlier stories showed them as mindless, selfish, over-sexed conjur-men, preaching hell fire and the golden streets of Glory Land, categorizing sin and salvation neatly and superficially, reveling in the applause of the crowds, shrewdly soliciting money from supporters, and at times seducing the females in the congregation. Peterkin pictures one preacher in *Black April* who is a womanizer, a thief, and a murderer, and yet is an enormously successful "spiritual leader." Green's preacher in "The Prayer Meeting" is not a bit better. And the preacher in *A Good Man* is the most repellent of all the Negro characters in the story. There are a couple of more sensitive studies of this Negro preacher-womanizer: Zora Neale Hurston's portrait of John Buddy in *Jonah's Gourd Vine* (a man whose flair for preaching is exceeded only by his weakness for women), and Nan Bagby Stephens' *Glory* (the story of a man who cannot resist seducing his parishioners).

More recent preachers have fared somewhat better with the authors. The minister in Carter's *Winds of Fear* is a bit too much of an Uncle Tom for Carter, but he is no buffoon or seducer either. He is simply too apologetic about his own race and too servile in his relations with whites. Like Ellison's Dr. Bledsoe, however, he is shrewd enough to realize the financial profit available from staying on good terms with whites. And Warren's minister in *The Flood* is one of the most intelligent and astute characters in the book. Of course, the most cynical portrayal of the modern Negro minister who uses his education and his position for his own ends appears in the Harlem section of *Invisible Man*. Rinehart is a Lothario with fast women, a bag man for the numbers racket, and a saint to his female parishioners. Numerous examples of the Daddy Faith, revival-type preacher also appear in modern novels, but are usually presented for the emotionalism of the service, the message of the sermon, or the exoticism of their regalia— not for their personalities. (*Lie Down in Darkness* has an especially rich example of this figure.)

Nat Turner is an effective portrait of a Negro minister. He knows scripture thoroughly and uses it as a guide for his life. He can outquote and outpreach most white ministers, who refuse him recognition because he has not an appropriate college diploma. Both the perverted Baptist who owns him briefly and the frozen-faced, cruelly dogmatic Episcopalian whom he eventually causes to be slaughtered have less personal committment to their religion than does he. Like modern race leaders, he finds the Old Testament prophets appealing for their activism and their anger at bondage and weakness. Coming to identify his people more and more with the Jews in Egypt or in Babylon, he thinks of himself as Moses or Jeremiah.

When confronted with Margaret Whitehead's gentle preference for the New Testament scriptures on love and brotherhood, he is disturbed. Rejecting her loving religion, he instigates a blood bath, of which he is at first only a nominal part. It is at Margaret's home, when Nat sees his "Godly" leadership is soon to be preempted by Godless black brutes, that he performs his only murder. In a moving and symbolic gesture, he stabs Margaret, whom he had dreamed of raping. And then, as an act of love in response to her cries of pain, he bashes her head in and relieves her agony. Her death has its atonement in his allowing another young girl to run to warn the farmers of the approaching black army. Through this acknowledge-ment of his sin and his willingness to fail, he dies, thinking of Margaret and the selfless love that she symbolized in her martyr's death. It is a beautifully handled relationship: the two bright young people, drawn to one another by their intelligence and tastes, and religion, and torn asunder by the social codes that would make their love unthinkable. She becomes the martyred saint through whom Nat is cleansed of his hatred and reconciled with his God as he goes stoically to his death.

Styron appears to be one of the rare modern writers concerned not simply with the Negro's profession as a minister, but with his adaptation of the Christian faith to his needs. Both in *Lie Down in Darkness* and in *The Confessions of Nat Turner*, he tries to see the means by which the Negro can make the white man's religion his own. Although concerned with a racial pattern of thought, Styron has no tendency to accept stereotyped, over-simplified answers to this complex theological and psychological puzzle.

Outside of the doctor, the preacher, and on much rarer occasions, the teacher (*Abraham's Bosom, Voice at the Back Door, Winds of Fear,* and *The Store* all have examples), the most influential figure in the Negro community is the Negro undertaker. He serves as the central character in *The Liberation of Lord Byron Jones* as, dressed in funereal garb, he displays an undeviating intensity and integrity. A more human but less powerful version is to be found in the Negro leader of Arthur Gordon's *Reprisal,* where the undertaker's importance is explained: "In a smallish Southern town," says one character about the undertaker, "he is just about the most important person there is on that side of the color line. More important than the preacher, even." And then he explains why—"He has a telephone, as a rule—that makes him a kind of message center. And he's on pretty intimate terms with his people. Anything goes on, he knows about it. In fact . . . comes the black revolution, down here, the small-town undertakers will be the commissars." Wright also pictures an influential undertaker, (in *The Long Dream*) but his success is based on pay-offs to corrupt politicians and policemen, ownership of slum housing, and profits from bars and prostitutes. The undertaking is only the cover for his numerous rackets. Nor is he "educated" by any ordinary standards or definitions.

The educated Negro may not be able to work as a professional. In fact, if he returns to the South, he may expect to be a domestic servant in spite of his education (witness the college-educated Negro servants in *Strange Fruit* or *Birthright*). Or he may have to serve in this capacity while working for an education—as Beck Dozier's father did (*Voice at the Back Door*) or the young Negro serving the family in Warren's *At Heaven's Gate*, or the Negro scholar framed for the hit-and-run killing in Glasgow's *In This Our Life*.

Most of them find that the South offers no encouragement and little opportunity for education and personal progress. The majority of the Negroes in Southern fiction go North for their schooling, and in some cases even venture to Europe where, in hopes of escaping prejudice, they are tempted to remain as expatriates. Especially if the young Negro intellectual aspires to a field so remote from usual Negro prospects as literature, he finds that neither blacks nor whites can sympathize with his choice. Negroes generally understand any ambition to join the black bourgeoisie, that select community of Negroes who have succeeded by hard work and study (as Turpin's characters often do). But to choose to become a poet or novelist, Wright discovered, elicits only an aghast "Who on earth put such ideas into your nigger head?" Wright saw that to stay in the South meant, for him, to "submit to live the life of a genial slave" or to "thrust the whites out of my mind, forget them; and find release from anxiety and longing in sex and alcohol."

The Negro professional could return South, but to do so meant and often still means that he must be prepared to conform: he would be unwise to make his house attractive from the outside, he must expect to live in niggertown, probably in a run-down rented home which the white landlord refuses to improve. (The recent novel *Birthright* points out purely physical problems of a Negro's desiring an attractive home built on land that he owns himself.) He must expect that he can not take his family to a first-class restaurant, or to a movie or a play (unless he is willing to sit in the Negro gallery); he may not call a white taxi or sit in the front of a bus or even expect a decent education for his children.[6] (Note that recent social changes should soon be reflected in literature so that these problems become less sizeable or disappear altogether.) In addition, the educated Negro should expect occasional personal insults against which he cannot defend himself; and even worse, he must expect that his wife or children can be subject to insult or injury too. A Negro in *Reprisal*, for example, finds that vicious whites can break his child's balloon and humiliate the father in front of his child while he must remain docile and seemingly imperturbable.

So, to go South, one must have at least a touch of missionary zeal, if not a real case of masochism. Miss Anderson may preach in *Southbound* that, "Some of us must crusade for what we call rights, and some of us must crusade for the minds and bodies that will be able to make effective use of those rights," but we feel her heroine is sacrificing more than she realizes in order to undertake the crusade and return to her home. Sam, the doctor in *Strange Fruit*, also goes back because the South needs him, but he is subjected to insults by illiterate whites, his mother and his sweetheart are both raped by white men, and he is unable to lift a hand or even express publicly his indignation. Not surprisingly, most Negroes echo Richard Wright's powerful conclusion to his autobiography, *Black Boy*:

The white South said that it knew "niggers," and I was what the white South called a "nigger." Well, the white South had never known me— never known what I thought, what I felt. The white South said that I had a "place" in life. Well, I had never felt my "place"; or, rather, my deepest instincts had always made me reject the "place" to which the white South had assigned me. It had never occurred to me that I was in any way an inferior being. And no word that I had ever heard fall from the lips of southern white men had ever made me really doubt the worth of my own humanity. True, I had lied. I had stolen. I had struggled to contain my seething anger. I had fought. And it was perhaps a mere accident that I had never killed . . . . But in what other ways had the South allowed me to be natural, to be real, to be myself, except in rejection, rebellion, and aggression?

Not only had the southern whites not known me, but, more important still, as I had lived in the South I had not had the chance to learn who I was. The pressure of southern living kept me from being the kind of person that I might have been. I had been what my surroundings had demanded, what my family—conforming to the dictates of the whites above them—had expected of me, and what the whites had said that I must be. Never being fully able to be myself, I had slowly learned that the South could recognize but a part of a man, could accept but a fragment of his personality, and all the rest—the best and deepest things of heart and mind—were tossed away in blind ignorance and hate.

I was leaving the South to fling myself into the unknown, to meet other situations that would perhaps elicit from me other responses. And if I could meet enough of a different life, then, perhaps, gradually and slowly I might learn who I was, what I might be. I was not leaving the South to forget the South, but so that some day I might understand it, might come to know what its rigors had done to me, to its children. I fled so that the numbness of my defensive living might thaw out and let me feel the pain—years later and far away—of what living in the South had meant.

Yet, deep down, I knew that I could never really leave the South, for there had been slowly instilled into my personality and consciousness, black though I was, the culture of the South. So, in leaving, I was taking a part of the South to transplant in alien soil, to see if it could grow differently, if it could drink of new and cool rains, bend in strange winds, respond to the warmth of other suns, and, perhaps to bloom . . . . And if that miracle ever did happen, then I would know that there was yet hope in that southern swamp of despair and violence, that light could emerge even out of the blackest of the southern night. I would know that the South too could overcome its fear, its hate, its cowardice, its heritage of guilt and blood, its burden of anxiety and compulsive cruelty.

The first half of *Invisible Man* is a symbolic summary, instructive and artistic, of many of the patterns apparent in second- and third-rate novels. Ellison had the obvious advantage of voluminous interpretation to draw on for his own tightly packed collection of Negro nightmares. In the first part of *Invisible Man* the naive young hero is trying to follow the pattern of Booker T. Washington. (Later, when he has lived for a while in the North, he appears to prefer the more revolutionary W.E.B. Dubois.) Accepting at face value the encouragement of the white and the black community, he believes that he need only be humble and work hard in order to achieve success. The cynical advice of his shrewd old grandfather ("overcome 'em with yeses, undermine 'em with grins, agree 'em to death and destruction,") confuses him and leads him to suspect a treachery in his own model deportment. But his endeavors are sincere, if suspect to the other black boys watching him angrily. He gives the proper speech for high school graduation, feels the proper pride at being asked to repeat it at a white businessmen's banquet, demeans himself properly by taking part in a battle royal first, swallows his blood while properly delivering his humble speech to the jeering, drunken men, and (after one Freudian slip suggesting subconscious angers) wins his reward—a scholarship to a Negro college.

There he continues his ritualistic path: he ingratiates himself with the school administrators, follows the rules, and never questions the system. In his Horatio Alger world, he believes he will become a great educator, like Bledsoe and the founder, a liberator of his people. The campus statue of the founder does bother him faintly since he can not decide the nature of its symbolic action:

In my mind's eye I see the bronze statue of the college Founder, the cold Father symbol, his hands outstretched in the breathtaking gesture of lifting a veil that flutters in hard, metallic folds above the face of the kneeling slave; and I am standing puzzled, unable to

decide whether the veil is really being lifted, or lowered more firmly
in place; whether I am witnessing a revelation or a more efficient
blinding.

Education, as he has known it in the South, is a barrier
to understanding the real world. This the invisible hero
discovers when he is asked to chauffeur Mr. Norton, a
white trustee, during a visit to the campus. Instead of
realizing that a Southern Negro survives by convincing the
white man he has what he wants rather than by actually
giving it to him, the boy follows directions blindly. This
leads him first to driving the man to the old slave-quarters,
a slum area carefully hidden before from this philanthropist who so enjoys feeling that his money has erased such
illiteracy and degradation. After a traumatic discussion
with the incestuous Jim Trueblood, Norton has a stroke.
Again the unwitting boy follows directions too forth-
rightly. When asked to find Mr. Norton a drink, he drives
him to an off-limits saloon, the Golden Day. Here Norton
witnesses the reverse horror of Southern illiteracy; insane
veterans, graduates of the ruinous Negro educational
system, are in control of the saloon while their super-ego
(Supercargo) is upstairs with a prostitute. A Negro doctor
diagnoses Norton's condition, displaying his professional
ability in doing so. But he also reveals that his education
has brought him only pain. To be educated and to be a
Negro is madness. The vet says to the frightened and
confused Norton: "To some you are the great white
father, to others the lyncher of souls, but for all, you are
confusion come even into the Golden Day." Having been
beaten with whips for saving a human life, the doctor-
veteran, has lifted the veil of blindness from his own eyes
and has looked into the glaring light of the golden
day—which proves to be chaos, a prelude to madness. It is
no wonder that Bledsoe, the shrewd manager of white

men's myths, must rid the campus of his blind young student. The boy is a threat to the entire system because of his innocence and idealism.

The wit of Ralph Ellison's cynical vision of education in the South contrasts powerfully with the more involved and emotional tone of Richard Wright's. While both are writing from their own experiences, it is obvious that Wright's experiences were far more lacerating than Ellison's. The superiority of Ellison's novel to Wright's autobiography lies largely in the greater distance Ellison has achieved. By a series of symbolic scenes, he has structured his life into the more universal pattern of art. Carefully withholding information and judgment until it is organically relevant, he allows the reader to develop through the hero's experiences. Therefore, although the hero is a bit of a Sambo, and clearly a type (or archetype) of Southern Negro, he is no stereotype. Out of the whole catalogue of recent Southern novels dealing with the problems of the educated Negro in the modern South, only Ellison's is likely to be long remembered.

To stay and become a martyr, or to leave and find a lonely release, these were the alternatives for the aggressive young Negro until World War II. But Richard Wright's anger was echoing in too many minds for the situation to remain stagnant. While many of the more energetic and intelligent Negroes were leaving the South, a new Southern leadership, drawn largely from among educators and churchmen, was developing that was to mobilize the Southern Negroes' angers and frustrations.

Since the Civil War and even before, the specter haunting the white man was the brute Negro—a stereotype drawn from the powerfully built Negroes who loomed as a perpetual menace to the white-dominated South. Presented in Dixon's fiction as an unreasoning animal, he was the classic "bad nigger," the one lynch-law was supposedly designed to control. White artists could not explore the motives for his fury without admitting the injustices of the Southern system they preferred to ignore. Thomas Dixon had shown this brute Negro in Reconstruction days swaggering about in his new-found, unwisely conferred freedom, contradicting, insulting, and assaulting austerely dignified landed white aristocrats. For an author like Dixon, this stereotyped character was the justification for the Klan and for lynch-law. Unlike his contented brethren, he knew no loyalty to his white benefactors, no respect for frail white virgins—had no sense of his "place." He was an egotistic, sex-driven, power-hungry perversion of humanity.

Later authors, recognizing the old melodramatic villain in the stereotype, tended to discard it as unwarranted. Faulkner uses some disloyal slaves, and shows obvious distaste for their antics, but he displays none of the negrophobia of Dixon's *The Clansman*. When, in the 'twenties and 'thirties, villains appeared in Julia Peterkin's or DuBose Heyward's stories, they were merely selfish or violent—not apelike. And their anger was directed against other Negroes (as Ellison says is the pattern developed by the battle-royal tactics of the Southern whites.) Styron is one of the few moderns who has dared to revive the character, presenting him in his original context, but showing how he became so brutish.

White men feared a possible flourishing of violent Negroes after World War I; W.E.B. DuBois spoke of "the pale ghost of fear which Negro soldiers call up in the white South." But, as we saw earlier, the more aggressive Negroes returning from the war saw the perils of being lynched if they stayed in the South, and saw the jobs and opportunities if they went North. So most followed Richard

Wright's formula and left for new territory. With or without education, these heretofore "bad niggers" became more interesting to authors as the key to change within the Negro community. Wright's *Native Son* was a real breakthrough in explaining the frustrations and warping influences of Negro life that can turn the youth into the brute. Bigger Thomas is presented as a type of Negro, but not as the unconvincing brute stereotype. It is an interesting and sympathetic portrait of an anti-social type. In a country where manhood has been systematically symbolized by power, the Negro has come to equate the two. More than once, Wright has his Negro heroes pick up a gun and kill in order to prove their manliness. Faced with the alternatives of victimization or violence, Bigger may elect the latter without thought or malice. In Wright's careful sociological and psychological preparation of Bigger Thomas, he establishes the motivation for his villainy. The murder, dismemberment, and incineration of his white benefactors are acts motivated by fear. The violence he turns against his Negro paramour is a perverse love-hatred, confused by flight, fear, and anger. Wright's remarkable feat in *Native Son* lies in making the reader shudder at the violence and yet sympathize with the frightened young protagonist.

This virile young Negro, given to overt expression of his rage, became increasingly popular in fiction of the 'forties. The war helped to unite the physically powerful Negro with the intellectually alert Negro leader. Such authors as Witter Bynner (*Defeat*) and John Oliver Killens (*And Then We Heard the Thunder*) describe the outrage felt by Negro recruits serving in the Armed Forces. The war, fought ostensibly in the name of the Four Freedoms, managed to preserve segregation, to limit the role of the Negro largely to man-servant or construction-laborer, to humiliate the Negro serviceman wherever possible.

Killens describes the racial explosion that occurred in Brisbane, Australia, in 1943, which was not by any means the only racial revolt in the Second World War. Apparently there were thousands of spontaneous and individual rebellions, and white officers who led Negro soldiers into battle were often killed, the death being attributed to "combat." John Williams' *Sissie* portrays a Negro killing a brutal "cracker" over an insignificant issue. Really though, the death blow was struck as the Negro explains, "because he wouldn't let me live." The Negro learned in the Second World War that aggressiveness can pay dividends, that white men are not willing to be any more generous than they must be, that actual performance does not conform to touted ideals, that the Negro has power (in the white man's fear of him) which he has never really exploited.

For the novelist, this strange new Negro returning from the war was hard to type. He may be the educated Negro, dating from Stribling's novels in the 'twenties, who uses the law to change his society. Novels such as *The Southerner* (Kiker), *The Number of Our Days* (Gwaltney), or *Birthright* (Rogers) use this black Anglo-Saxon. He talks without an accent, is aloof, cynical, and shrewd. His motives are pure and his triumph certain. As a compensatory stereotype, he is as unreal as the tough news-reporter or wise judge who usually accompanies him. *The White Band*, a story of white citizens councils in the South, is one of the best of these civil rights novels and has the smallest percentage of stereotyping. But for the most part the emotionalism of the modern scene inclines the author into structuring preachy Southern westerns with good guys triumphing over bad guys.

A liberal viewer like Hodding Carter can easily see some of the possible variations of the leader (in *Winds of Fear*): There is Dr. Stanley, educated in the North, deeply hurt by prejudice so that he is a tangle of psychic scars; he hates the South, the whites, the white man's Negroes, and himself. On the other hand, there is Preacher McCutcheon, an Uncle Tom, a leader who derives his power from his pulpit; he has control over Negro thought and sentiments as Dr. Stanley never does. (Negroes are instinctively embarrassed and ill at ease in Dr. Stanley's thunderous presence.) But he is too moderate to be of much service to his people. Professor Monroe is a compromise between the mealy-mouthed "white man's nigger" and the bitter race-agitator. He admires the great Negro Americans whose pictures decorate his school's walls; he works quietly and steadily for recognition for Negroes; he encourages middle-class virtues of hard work, frugality, and patience. In short, he is the perfect Southern liberal white's Negro—but in no sense the hero of the Northern liberal, who tends to be much more extreme in his ideas and activistic in his program. But these types are all too pat to be real, as the far more subtle and powerful Ellison creations prove.

The temptation has been to categorize all leaders as followers of Booker T. Washington or of W.E.B. DuBois. And because the situation is current and emotionally charged, when a white man tries to explore the machinations of the sinister Negro, he finds himself sounding bigoted or didactic. His character is either the cynical villain without depth or the cruel exploiter without motivation. More often, the white man is afraid to try to picture a bad Negro for fear his character will be simply brute Negro. In *Invisible Man*, Ellison uses his knowledge of the Negro (which is apparently only available in such depth to the Negro himself—being "blood knowledge") to explore with penetration the many faces of Negroid evil—the cynical Uncle Tomism of the power-hungry educator, Bledsoe; the crude violence of the Harlem racist, Ras; the many-sided but empty shell of the con-man, Rinehart. The anger, selfishness, violence, cruelty, guile— the sinister deadly sins available to modern man are portrayed in Ellison's vision of the black man's hell. The writing is much more powerful than Carter's or Stribling's or Heyward's or Peterkin's or even Wright's, the psychology much richer and subtler. By comparison, Lillian Smith's *Strange Fruit* looks like an ill-prepared sociological tract and her concept of Negro psychology suitable for the wooden figures in a puppet show. In his black man's *Candide*, Ellison redefines modern man as well as the modern Negro. His Negro leaders may be cynical and selfish, but his black hero is the man who really matters; and he is innocent and benevolent and believing—at least at first—and still willing to learn and to make darkness grow visible even at the last.

Faulkner had pictured a banty-rooster Caspey after World War I, but he showed a Negro war hero after World War II. The Negro who steps out of the modern novel is not the cringing victim so typical of the 'twenties and the 'thirties. He often knows and uses the law in his own defense. Beck Dozier in Spencer's novel is so self-assured that he even dares to frame the sheriff. More and more educated, strong, sensitive, self-assured Negroes are emerging from the pages of Southern fiction. And these are the characters who offer the greatest challenge to the contemporary novelist.

William Styron's *The Confessions of Nat Turner* relates the new aggressive, virile, rebellious Negro of black power and urban riots and civil rights demonstrations to an historical personage. Styron, who studied the career of this rebel leader in an effort to understand him and his race, found that Nat broke up all the old patterns. Although

well treated, and seldom over-worked, he hated his white
masters and his slave condition. Although educated, he did
not reject the illiterate field hands nor their simple faith.
Nor was he motivated in any large measure by pure reason.
Tantalized by a hope for freedom and then disappointed,
he was consumed with the need to destroy. His fierce pride
could not allow him to return servile affection for the
thoughtless kindness of white people. And his anguished
love for his race made him hate their complacency, their
willingness to trade manhood for an animal-level of
subsistence. He is a study of a type—not simply a brute,
nor simply an intellect—but the man of feeling, of manly
pride, of prophetic zeal who is filled with a hunger and a
vision. Such a study would have meant little to a
Reconstruction audience or one looking for the intellectual delights of a Negro renaissance. But in an age when even
the Southerner finds the Negro unpredictable and his mask
being replaced with unbelievable emotions, Nat is an
enormously relevant study as well as an aesthetically
pleasing and psychologically subtle one. Styron is not
afraid to make his hero sexual, lusting after white women
as well as black. He uses an axe for a murder weapon
without seeing the axe as a "nigger" weapon; he is
physically powerful without being a brute, lusty without
being animalistic. With all of the brute Negro characteristics, Nat yet becomes a revealing and individualized
portrait.

The new Negro of fiction is a man who is less than
enthusiastic about fighting what he considers white man's
wars; he is cynical of white liberals and moderates; he may
even be a black racist, a civil rights agitator, or a member
of the black proletariat; he is usually sensitive to belittling
nomenclature and prejudiced responses. He may be
ashamed of his own desires—for cornpone or chitterlings or

blackeyed peas or jazz or flashy clothes—because he is enormously self-conscious about his image; he may hate himself and he may be embarked on a futile search for identity.

His struggle now is for identity: what DuBois knows as a sense of never being heard, and Ellison sees as the sense of never being seen, and James Baldwin calls not knowing his name. All of these are really the Negro's response to the unpleasant and untrue image projected by his world, purporting to be him and yet so clearly not him that in time he comes to wonder whether he does indeed exist at all.[7] Instead of the old graces of submission and endurance, the modern Negro character needs self-knowledge and flexibility. He may be in fact the exact opposite of the old stereotype of the Negro as happy, religious, content, lusty, musical, etc. Ellison's hero is not a stereotype but the existential man:

> For even as his life toughens the Negro [says Ellison], even as it brutalizes him, sensitizes him, dulls him, goads him to anger, moves him to irony, sometimes fracturing and sometimes affirming his hopes; even as it shapes his attitudes toward family, sex, love, religion; even as it modulates his humor, tempers his joy—it *conditions* him to deal with his life and with himself. Because it is *his* life and no mere abstraction in someone's head. He must live it and try consciously to grasp its complexity until he can change it; must live it *as* he changes it. He is no mere product of his socio-political predicament. He is the product of the interaction between his racial predicament, his individual will and the broader American cultural freedom in which he finds his ambiguous existence. Thus he, too, in a limited way, is his own creation.

Ellison points to the day when we will look at the Negro not as the Negro, but a man. But Ellison knows that being a man involves accepting one's own heritage, and therefore being a specific type of man—one with black skin, kinky hair, taste for music, nostalgia and hatred for the South, or even a love of yams. He says of his invisible man that he wants to be visible, but not colorless.

It is instructive to see how literary tastes have changed over the past century, in large part reflecting changes in attitudes. For the new Southern Negro is in reality a new look at the old brute negro—where he was "animalistic," now he is virile; where he was "ungrateful," now he is independent; and where he was "uppity," now he is self-assured. But the good artist still has the task of sorting the characteristics out to build a man who is both individual and typical. His present temptation will be to conform to modern compensatory stereotypes, making of his hero a black Sir Charles Grandison.

9

TYPICAL PATTERNS

As we have seen, the Southerner is obsessed with the
Negro—that black shadow across the Southland. His very
blackness disturbs the white man, for in white mythology
black is the essence of evil, the symbol of mystery, of the
unknown and unknowable. The white man loves, hates,
fears, despises, admires, and envies the Negro—but he
cannot ignore him. The Negro is omnipresent to cloud his
conscience, to upset his economic system, to challenge his
manhood, to threaten his power structure. Historically, the
Southerner had not merely enslaved, exploited, raped, and
lynched the Negro, he has also befriended him, supported
him, confided in him, shared his black mother's milk and
affection, and loved his black mistress and his black friend
with all his heart. In constant contact with the black man,
claiming intimate knowledge of "The Negro," he is actually
ignorant of large areas of Negro thought and life. His very
claim to knowledge of this mythological Negro is evidence
of his ignorance. He often generalizes from his limited
knowledge of a small group of Negroes and assumes the
generalizations to be universally valid. One of the great
fonts of Southern literature has been the Southern woman
who revels in telling the world about the "real Negro" on
the basis of her experience with her cook and handyman.

The writer of fiction in the South finds that he cannot
omit the Negro from his stories, but the more sensitive

is racked with suspicions that his comments on the Negro are fatuous. It is patently obvious that the white man cannot understand what it is to live in black skin—even Griffin's experiment of dyeing the skin is not the same thing. No experience in white existence qualifies as precisely parallel, and the writer's imagination inclines to belittle or magnify the slights, the joys, the angers, or the dreams of his Negro characters. The handicap is all the more pronounced as a result of the reticence that the Southern Negro cultivates so that he may survive in a hostile environment. Perhaps the mask quality so often apparent in novels dealing with black and white relations is an honest replica of the life situation. For the social patterns of Southern life require such thoroughly codified behavior by both races in integrated situations that it would be virtually impossible to know much of Negro thought from normal relationships. Even the testimony of Negro friends is not altogether trustworthy; at any time, the confidant may be merely echoing those sentiments that he senses his white friend desires to hear and that he himself has been taught to mouth.

Verisimilitude is further muddled by the need of the author to find an audience and a publisher. He may write what he believes his audience wishes to hear and what is likely to be published by a Northern press. As Hubbell comments, most readers of Southern fiction live outside of the South, "a fact that makes this fiction for an alien audience, forcing the writer to conform to their tastes and to exploit the peculiar elements of his own region."[1] In one period, the Negro as ape may draw a large audience; in another, the Negro as folk hero or exotic primitive entertains the available readers of fiction. Our day seems to demand the Negro as victim, as Freudian sex symbol, or as angry young iconoclast. The Negro's role in society may be changing from hewer of wood to carrier of banners, but the metamorphosis in literature also reflects an effort to conform to the tastes of the reading public. And, in addition, the artist, although he may not pose as a sociologist, does inevitably react to the intellectual and social forces that impinge upon his private and public world. His work must perforce reflect or refute the attitudes of his day.

The critic becomes particularly aware, in reading novels dealing with current social problems, that however significant the moral of a problem novel may be, the writer must be wary of producing pure propaganda. He remains an artist only so long as he refuses to allow his thesis to snare him into writing a tract. When he turns entirely to polemics, he must be judged for his authority and veracity in his newly elected field of endeavor—politics, sociology, anthropology, etc.—and is no longer under consideration solely as an artist.

Most of our major Southern writers have finally succumbed to this temptation of turning social critic, especially on the Negro question, and have stepped forward with forthright, enthusiastic, sincere, but essentially inartistic tracts. Faulkner was an inveterate letter writer and speech maker on this subject; Robert Penn Warren has written *Segregation: The Inner Conflict in the South* and *Who speaks for the Negro?*; Erskine Caldwell's *In Search of Bisco* is a quasi-artistic tract on the plight of the Negro in the South; and Lillian Smith, who made her position crystal clear in *Strange Fruit*, has felt obliged to thrust her point home again in such unadulterated polemics as *Now Is the Time* and *Killers of the Dream*.

The problem involved here is the dual personality of the artist. In troubled times, one feels sorely tempted to stand up and be counted, speaking in *sua persona*, overtly and

distinctly. This temptation may well override the awareness that one may not be qualified to serve as spokesman
for the South, for the Negro, or even for the liberal
community. The artists, in short, are transferring a prestige
won for aesthetic ability to an area in which aesthetic
ability is irrelevant. If the artist feels, as he usually does,
that the end justifies the means, he goes ahead and adds to
the mountains of fervent but repetitive pleas for integration and love.

Miss Smith, however, is different. So concerned was she
with her thesis in *Strange Fruit* that she built a modern
fable of miscegenation and victimization out of cardboard
characters and make-believe scenery. In doing so she
followed the Wright school of novelists who have most
often succumbed to the temptation always luring the
writer of the Southern Negro-oriented novel. When a
dedicated champion of justice writes about the Southern
Negro, he is hard-put to produce a creditable work of art.
The fraudulent ending of Attaway's fine novel *Blood on
the Forge* is another example of the art-vs.-message
problem. The organic unity of a work is destroyed by the
conscious manipulation of situation and characterization
for socially applaudable purposes. Most of the works of
the 'thirties serve as illustrations of this same criticism. The
artist is constantly tempted to become an essayist or a
journalist, crusading but hardly immortal. Ralph Ellison
had indicated that one of the major problems facing the
Negro writer is the assimilation of his life into his art so
that, refraining from writing propaganda, he instead
transforms the stuff of his existence into literature. James
Baldwin is an example of a Negro who finds this difficult
to manage; Richard Wright is an example of one who is
occasionally able to transform his most tortured thoughts
into living characters. Other Negro novelists have stumbled

on other ways, choosing to write all-Negro novels, all-white novels, or assimilative novels in which race is not at issue. But each of these techniques may quickly become a pose and a means of avoiding the heart of the matter.

Considering all these problems—that a work of art is seldom a valid sociological study; that the Southern white writer must write about areas of Negro thought and life of which he is partially ignorant; that the Negro writer is usually too close to the tensions of existence to transform his life into powerful fiction; that, black or white, the writer must adapt to a public and to a publisher; and that the fads of the day influence not only what is accepted but also what one is inspired to write—in spite of all these negative factors, the explicit and implicit comments of modern Southern novelists on the subject of the Negro form a revealing pattern.

Surely art is not sociology. The good artist demonstrates his faith rather than stating it and footnoting it. The artist can dramatize a situation so that it moves many more people to compassion or wrath than will any number of statistical tables and revealing charts on lynch or rape. The artist may explore the Negro existentially rather than cataloguing his background, mental capacity, and emotional stability in a colorless case study. Ralph Ellison can tell us more about Negro leadership than Gunnar Myrdal could ever hope to do. And William Faulkner can show us more of the mind of the South than W.J. Cash could imagine exists. For those upon whom nothing is lost, these authors offer insights more powerful, though less explicit, than any collection of sociological, historical, psychological, or anthropological papers. Such men write as individuals and may not therefore be so universal as we would wish, but as they echo one another they do reveal a large number of trends—especially in their comments on Negroes. They are, for the most part, more liberal in their ideas than are most Southerners, but then they are writing for a preponderantly Northern audience and may be accommodating themselves slightly (if not outrageously) to that audience, thereby serving as "imperfect mirrors" at best. Artists are not typical people; such a study as this cannot be used to comment on all Southerners—only on some of the better Southern writers of fiction.

In fact, some of the Southerners who have achieved the greatest success in recent years have cultivated not stereotypes but eccentrics, Truman Capote, Eudora Welty, Carson McCullers, and Tennessee Williams, for example. We are not the least surprised that Capote's Negro cook claims she is an Indian and stuffs her toothless mouth full of cotton wadding, or that Welty's Negro was the "Geek" in the circus, or that McCullers' Negro doctor becomes a Communist and drives his family away from him because of the intensity of his love, or that Tennessee Williams' sadistic Negro masseur beats and eats the pitiful little white masochist. The only patterns one might expect from such authors is a consistent inconsistency. The gothic, the grotesque, the eccentric Southern novelist, however, is less inclined to write about Negroes since he finds ample subject matter among decadent white Southern aristocrats. As a rule, in the midst of the Southern gothic world, the Negro characters lend an air of stability and common sense.

Several patterns of thought do emerge, appearing even in the better Southern novels. For example, most authors concur with Faulkner in his amazement at the Negro's ability to endure—to take more than whites. This characteristic peculiar to an oppressed people is one of the obvious parallels with the Jews that has proven useful in Negro sermons. Able to survive servitude and cruelty with apparent equanimity and even occasional good humor, Negroes confuse authors trying to analyze their dark laughter. Warren suspects that the laughter is a shrewdly designed mask. Faulkner feels it may hide nothing more complex than stupidity. Styron believes it is the hysterical response of a people who have little alternative.

Ellison, like Warren, suggests that the laughter disguises pain and serves as a mode of survival. In an essay on "Richard Wright's Blues," Ellison describes the alternatives available to Wright and his contemporaries in the South:

> In the South of Wright's childhood there were three general ways for Negroes to survive: They could accept the role created for them by the whites and perpetually resolve the resulting conflicts through the hope and emotional catharsis of Negro religion; they could repress their dislike of Jim Crow social relations while striving for the middle way of respectability, becoming—consciously or unconsciously—the accomplices of the whites in oppressing their brothers; or they could reject the situation, adopt a criminal attitude, and carry on an unceasing psychological scrimmage with the whites, which often flared forth into physical violence.

From Ellison's viewpoint, both "good niggers" and "bad niggers" of earlier days were adjusting to the same problem of frustration. One expressed it in violence, usually against other Negroes, while the other channeled it into religious ecstasy. But the frustration remains and may break out in the most well-adjusted Negro in a sudden, inexplicable act of violence or in rebellion by his children.

The Southerner is generally aware of certain contradictions in Negro character. He knows that a good Negro may be cleaner than a bad one, or less lazy, or gentler with children, while he may have a better sense of humor, and may sing spirituals rather than blues, and go regularly to church. But he may have no sexual morality, he may steal or lie, and he may be as wild as the next Negro on a

Saturday night. He may be cruel to his own children and disloyal to his own race. Still, if he is gentle with his white folks and loyal to them, they see him as a "good nigger."

Ellison has commented that this frequently touted loyalty to whites, "given where one's humanity is unrecognized," seems a bit obscene. Recently a few novelists have radically transformed this loyalty theme. The modern Negro hero establishes his manhood by insulting and betraying whites. One interesting example of this is in Julian Meade's *The Back Door*, a realistic and moving story of the late 'thirties that tells of an intelligent, hard-working young Negro maid, who reacts angrily to the insults and accusations of her white employers. Although she has been scrupulously honest in her dealings with them, they accuse her of lying and stealing. Feeling that she cannot accept their evaluation of her and retain any self-respect, she protests her innocence and leaves her job. In the climactic action she achieves dignity and a moral victory—as well as consequent destitution and heartbreak. Her victory is Pyrrhic at best. But even at the frightful price she eventually pays for her heroism (unemployment, hunger, poverty, pain), we feel that she has made the only possible choice. So the characteristics of the "uppity" Negro are here transformed into the characteristics of the heroic Negro. As novelists grow increasingly liberal, this reversal of values and the disintegration of the slave character make the old loyalty of the plantation darkies seem increasingly repugnant. We begin to suspect that Loosh, the villain Negro in Faulkner's *The Unvanquished*, has every right to turn against his Southern owners during the Civil War. And we come to admire honest disloyalty as we once admired unthinking loyalty. The liberal novelists now must, in fact, be alert to the problems of the anti-stereotype stereotype.

The older portrait of the good, loyal darky also included

his preference for servitude. After the Civil War he was characteristically the Negro who stayed on the plantation, not to be lured by the promises of carpetbaggers, not to become the miserable freeman who populated the cities. Later, he became the hard-working share-cropper, still remaining in bondage to the land and to his white folks, still ignoring the blandishments of scallawags and Yankees. Nat Turner finds only a handful of Negroes will rebel, in spite of their harsh treatment. His defeat, in fact, comes at the hands of Negroes fighting for the white landowners. To the Southerner, this good Negro's rejection of freedom indicates his basic wisdom and his admission that his race is too infantile and inexperienced to face the responsibilities of freedom. Over and over we are told how child-like the Negroes on the plantations were, and how child-like most of the freemen still are. The white-haired Southern aristocrat is allowed to reply sneeringly to abolitionist propaganda with such platitudes as : "Free? I wish I could be free!" The venerable white father-of-his-people then furrows his classic brow and returns to his oak-paneled study where he worries over how he will feed his helpless and almost useless child-slaves. Again Faulkner's *The Unvanquished* is a case in point, as well as Frances Gaither's *Follow the Drinking Gourd*. The Negro, or at least, the bad Negro, may want freedom, but the Southerner knows that he is not ready for it.

Faulkner dramatizes this frequently reiterated platitude in his story of the ex-slave girl who marries the Northern educated Negro and moves with him to a barren Arkansas farm. The Negro husband considers farm labor demeaning, even though the alternative is poverty and starvation. Luckily for the irresponsible and ignorant pair, Ike McCaslin takes it upon himself to provide for their basic needs, turning the other cheek to their crass ingratitude and arrogance. Ovid Williams Pierce is one of many Southern novelists who chronicle similar scenes (undoubtedly with some basis in fact): The Negroes abandoning their cabins and their work and their families after the Civil War, rambling along roads in search of the River Jordan and a work-less utopia, often being sent home by confused and irate Yankee officers. T.S. Stribling shows later scenes of carpetbagger politicians supporting free-loading Negroes on government hand-outs, encouraging their shiftless and irresponsible ways. Repeatedly, the Reconstruction Negro is pictured as irresponsible, infantile, incompetent, confused, ignorant—in short, thoroughly unprepared for freedom.

Some of the modern novelists who have examined the Civil War and post-Civil War scene have explored the idea that the Negro confuses freedom with license. Robert Penn Warren works over this point at some length in *Band of Angels*. And another modern, Edward Kimbrough, sees the problem as the need to participate in one's own emancipation. In this sense, the Civil Rights struggle is seen as a second Civil War in which the Negro has a chance to help free himself from bondage. On the other hand, Douglas Kiker, another socially conscious modern writer, seems to reject this view. When a white man suggests that Negroes deserve their situation because of their notorious crime rate, filth, extravagance, sexual abandon, and destruction of property, the Negro attorney in Kiker's *The Southerner* replies that this argument is irrelevant; in a democracy a man does not need to earn his freedom. It is not a matter of deserving, it is a matter of birth. But the speculation still goes on: whether the Negro understands or deserves equality, whether any man can ever be truly free, whether there are discernible limits to freedom, etc.

Even after Civil War and Reconstruction novels declined

temporarily in popularity, the slave characteristics still lived on in the faithful servants. The cook or handyman is usually naturally happy, has innate abilities as a story-teller, and is an excellent natural musician. Because it reeks of its relationship to the old slave stereotype, the faithful retainer character is also falling into disrepute these days. Modern Negro characters are often as sullen as old-time "bad niggers"; they are often taciturn in their responses to whites, refusing to ape garrulous old Uncle Remus.

While the musical ability was at one time used as proof of the immediacy of slave ancestry, it is now most often cited as an admirable and exotic quality. Heroines with musical ability, however, refuse to indulge themselves in crooning Negro spirituals (Heyward's Mamba was one of the last of the spiritual singers), and they turn instead to cultivated musical expression. David Westheimer (in *Summer on the Water*) has his mulatto heroine sing only classical songs when she is alone; Barbara Anderson (in *Southbound*) has her heroine study classical music in Europe; and Mrs. L.M. Alexander (in *Candy*) sends her brown beauty to Harlem as an exotic dancer. (Heyward anticipated all of this by making Mamba's granddaughter became a concert soloist, combining the spirituals, blues, and classics in her celebrated concerts.) That the Negro has an inborn talent for music is so generally accepted that the aunt of the quadroon boy in Edith Pope's *Colcorton* is afraid that the child's response to rhythm will mark him as a Negro. Strangely enough, considering that jazz is the product of the Southern Negro, the jazz musician is seldom used by Southern authors. Eudora Welty pictures a Negro jazz musician in "Powerhouse" (in *A Curtain of Green and Other Stories*) but she does not integrate him into a story. Thus, because of the echoes of the old slave stereotype, the modern author reacts with compensatory stereotypes, refusing to allow his Negro characters to chuckle, to ramble on in folksy tales, or to sing spirituals. The contrary stereotype is often as pretentious and dreary as Uncle Tom himself.

The modern is also somewhat afraid to attribute violence to his Negro characters. When a modern Negro is accused of a serious crime, the author pictures him as the innocent victim of an all-white jury or a lynch mob. Even in the altercations with other members of his race, he is less violent than in the novels of the 'twenties and 'thirties. Scenes of razor fights are becoming so infrequent that, when Elizabeth Spencer describes a razor-slashing scene in *Voice at the Back Door*, the reader is suspicious. The action seems out of character for the cerebral, cynical Negro involved; and as it turns out, the story is indeed a fabrication. In the folksier novels of the 'twenties and 'thirties, razor battles were a frequent component of drinking and dancing scenes. George Wylie Henderson's *Ollie Miss* has a scene of slashing provoked by a difference of opinion over a girl's selection of a dancing partner. And Julia Peterkin's characters are in constant razor battles—in *Black April* even the Negro preacher has razor scars. Since these fights were a part of the exotic Negro Saturday night, full of drunken, lusty abandon so popular with earlier novelists, they would necessarily disappear in the modern treatment of the Negro.

Less and less is being said about the gargantuan sexual appetite and prowess of the Negro (which did so much in earlier days to establish the stereotype of the brute Negro); and in some of the more recent scenes of sexual temptation, the Negro finds himself either impotent or at least unaroused. The promiscuity of the Negro characters is somewhat less typical than formerly, and certainly not handled as such a ludicrous characteristic. Julia Peterkin, for example, twice had her Negroes murmur sympathetically that an illegitimate child is a "slip" to be expected of a young girl. Scarlet Sister Mary and Candy are being replaced by demure young ladies striving as valiantly as any mid-Victorian heroine to preserve their chastity in the face of overwhelming odds.

The emotionalism of the Negro, so long a platitude of characterization, has also undergone some alteration in modern novels. In fact, Richard Wright insists that the Negro is not actually emotional at all. In his autobiography, *Black Boy*, he speculates on the insensitivity of his people:

> I used to mull over the strange absence of real kindness in Negroes, how unstable was our tenderness, how lacking in genuine passion we were, how void of great hope, how timid our joy, how bare our traditions, how hollow our memories, how lacking we were in those intangible sentiments that bind man to man, and how shallow was even our despair. After I had learned other ways of life I used to brood upon the unconscious irony of those who felt that Negroes led so passionate an existence! I saw that what had been taken for our emotional strength was our negative confusions, our flights, our fears, our frenzy under pressure.

In such commentaries, Wright has opened up a whole new interpretation of Negro psychology. The Uncle Tom, replaced by the Bigger Thomas, becomes the new Negro, and finally, perhaps, the existential Negro.

The religious zeal of the Negro character is also on the decline. Novels of the 'twenties and 'thirties made frequent mention of emotionally charged religious services, but the educated Negroes were even then withdrawing from such scenes. Waters Turpin's *O Canaan!* portrays the same rejection of primitive evangelical religion by the educated or prosperous Negroes that Ellison and Baldwin notice. Such fervor is more often pictured now as the characteristic of low-class Negroes. But even in the earlier novels, some more discriminating writers were aware that the Negroes themselves often judged religious exhibitionism harshly. Paul Green shows this relation between religion and class in "Birth Night Supper," and Heyward shows it in *Mamba's Daughters*. The middle class Negroes of these stories reject as beneath them the primitive worship of the "field niggers." The traditional religion of the Negro, used with great effectiveness as background for Styron's *Lie Down in Darkness*, is becoming an anachronism. Often now the Negro goes to church, like Mamba's granddaughter, to meet the right people, to display a talent; or like the invisible man, to enjoy the music and the old-fashioned oratory. A number of writers appear to agree with Baldwin's implied thesis, in *Go Tell It on the Mountain*, that emotional religion is an escape for Negroes who anticipate no happiness or success in this world. The new Negro echoes McCullers' Negro doctor in *The Heart Is a Lonely Hunter*, who feels out of place among his family's superstition and bibliolatry and who searches for an economic rather than a mystic solution to his people's problems. The "white God" of slave literature is being replaced by a black God with kinky hair—and even more often by the unnamed but undeniable modern deity, Power.

Modern novelists are breaking up the old stereotypes in many different ways. Instead of seeing all Negroes as alike, differentiated only as to whether they are good or bad, some now see them as members of a class structure, some as products of a region (with different types found in New Orleans, North Carolina, etc.), and others as products of an educational and social system. Clearly the modern tendency is to see the Negro not as a natural anything, but as a blank tablet and a product of environment. Thus, increasingly, the most popular portrait is of the Negro who has been away from home long enough to develop a new outlook—on his people and his area. Modern authors find him useful just as Goldsmith's oriental visitor served as a fresh commentator on the mores of eighteenth-century England. Very probably, Negro stereotypes will in time become as obsolete as the old Machiavelian villain with his Italian accent or the comic Irishman with his alcoholic lyricism. The race-consciousness engendered by modern life makes the reader increasingly uncomfortable when confronted with derogatory stereotypes.

One interesting result of the reaction against the stereotype is the chronicle of the Negro's search for identity, so often isolated as the most important theme of modern Negro literature. Once the role-playing is abandoned, then the man has a time of self-consciousness when he is paralyzed for fear that any desire or action may be in conformity with the abandoned image. He wants a racial or cultural identity and is unsure how to attain it while avoiding the old cliches about his race. Carson McCullers' Dr. Copeland, in his pilgrimage to a new identity, finds the world outside of the accepted image to be a lonely one. And communication being what it is (especially in the McCullers' world), even those who agree with him and share his dreams do so in the wrong way or for the wrong reasons. Faulkner's Lucas Beauchamp is also such a man. By refusing to be a "nigger" he finds that he is not really anything. Actually, he is more McCaslin than anything else, but the McCaslins cannot acknowledge a Negro relative. He is aggressive in his effort to avoid the Negro pattern: It would be like a "nigger" to kill a white man, but Lucas is falsely accused of murder; if arrested, it would be like a "nigger" to roll his eyes and shake in fear of the lynch mob, but Lucas sets about calmly to prove his innocence; when freed, it would be like a "nigger" to grovel in dog-like devotion at the feet of the man who helped him, but Lucas haughtily demands to know the price of the help. Lucas, in short, refuses to be a "nigger." And, as a result, he often fails to be a human being. Ellison points to the perils of over-reacting to the derogatory stereotype. His hero is so afraid of reflecting Negroid tastes that he is afraid to eat pork chops for breakfast. His freedom comes when he admits that he likes yams dripping with butter and is not concerned with his image. He proclaims himself an unashamed chittlin' eater—and becomes a free man.

For the Southerner, role-playing is more important than for most other Americans: certain things are expected of women, of aristocrats, of poor-whites, of newspapermen, of bankers—even of members of any given family. Harper Lee points out that some Southerners believe they can predict or at least explain a person's behavior by fixing it in a family behavior pattern. Cleanth Brooks has explained much of Faulkner's stress on family and "blood" as a reflection of the Southern obsession with social relationships and codes of conduct.

When the Southerner is picturing the life around him, he is obliged to record some of this codification of roles. He is even confronted with the need to establish the type of the Southerner, a distinctive figure in American life. He thus finds himself saying that the Southerner carries with him the burden of his history: his knowledge of defeat, his defensive-shame about his role as slave-owner, his fury at the self-righteous, vengeful North, his agrarian tradition, his acquaintance with poverty, etc. But he recognizes that some Southerners are Tom Joads and others are Gavin Stevenses. Not all are Calvinists, not all condoned slavery, not all resent the North. While working with the type of

Southerner, the Southern novelist has been able to explore all of the diversity of Southern character as well. Gradually, he is also discovering the shadings of Negro humanity.

The modern novelist has fertile territory in his exploration of the Negro, but he has more traps to avoid and intricacies to master than ever before. No more can his pages flourish with flashing white grins, throaty voices saying, "Yassuh!" No more rolling of eyes and slapping of ample thighs in hearty laughter, no more crooning of spirituals to comfort lonely white children, no more Uncle Remus and Dilsey and Sambo. William Styron is now willing to look imaginatively into the history of the Negro rebel. He is able to contrast what Nat says with what he thinks, what people believe of him to what he really is. He is not tempted to decide between two stereotypes: the contented slave or the brute Negro. He can see that neither describes the probable pattern of psychology and action of the slave Nat Turner. Other writers and critics are growing increasingly aware of the subtleties of motivation and response available to the Negro.

The Negro-centered story continues to provide the able author with an exciting cluster of ideas and attitudes to explore. A number of excellent novels have already resulted from the fruitful combination of significant ability and diverse material. Even now the Southern white writer seldom makes his Negro character focal in his novel, and even the Negro writer seldom has an exclusively Negro tale to tell. When the authors tell their stories, they usually hesitate to use actual Negro speech because it is unintelligible to the larger part of the reading public. But even so, the Southern writer continues to return to the Negro, perhaps because books touching on the Negro are popular in the North, perhaps because he feels compelled to explain the Negro, or perhaps because he is participating in the Southern Negro-syndrome of guilt, anger, hatred, sympathy, and even love.

Some thirty years ago, after reading a large number of American novels by and about Negroes, Sterling Brown reported with some wrath that most Negro characters had been consciously or unconsciously stereotyped. His catalogue of stereotypes prevalent in the fiction of white writers is now clearly out of date, largely because the topics and prevailing forms have disappeared. Also, since that time, stereotyping has fallen in disfavor—or at least derogatory stereotyping. Changes in the Negroes' lives and aspirations, in their patterns of education and activity have been reflected by corresponding changes in their literary images. The old stereotypes have been re-formed or discarded. New ones, largely compensatory ones, have replaced them in new modes of fiction.

As novelists have grown enthusiastic about symbolism, Negroes have taken on greater symbolic implications: serving as the voice of wisdom, as primordial love, as Eden-innocence, as the dark unknown in man's heart and soul, as the sacrificial lamb or the scapegoat. In the novel of moral intensity, the Negro can represent the conscience or the guilt of mankind. In the novel of dislocation, the Negro can symbolize isolation, rootlessness, or invisibility. If, on the other hand, the novelist opts for realism or naturalism, there is still ample material in the sordid life of the Southern Negro mill-worker or share-cropper to delight the most lurid imagination. He can effectively focus on social injustice or on the bestiality of the average man by selecting his facts carefully and using the black Christ, the black cropper, or even the brute Negro for his hero. And, if the novelist is a Southern gothic enthusiast or an advocate of eccentric individualism, the Negro is as available as is the decadent Southern aristocrat for whimsical or blood-curdling exploitation.

There is no debate about the Negro's ubiquity or his utility. Whether symbolically or literally interpreted, the Negro is an invaluable character in the Southern novel. He is a part of the Southern landscape as well as the Southern psyche, and is therefore usually a natural enough component of Southern fiction. Artists have found that his presence can endow an otherwise drab scene with exotic appeal or local color. Even when used as nothing more than background for white action, the Negro is useful for contrast. If he speaks, his comments can bring the choric tone of an alien group looking with unclouded eyes at an involved situation. His silence can suggest mystery or disapproval. His gesture can suggest fear or pain or humor or wisdom. His endurance beyond the limits of the tragic action can make the anguish more moving, more meaningful, and more impressive. At a time of enormously complex reasoning and perversely contrived motivation, he can suggest a simple humane sanity.

As he moves closer to the center of the action, he becomes a more significant literary tool. Most often authors use the Negro as the touchstone by which they test value in character. Since the white man has, in the past, been able to torment the Negro with virtual impunity, his treatment of the Negro is a more valid indication of his nature than his action toward white men. The apparently shy man may rape a Negro woman brutally. The seemingly kind merchant may give the helpless Negro short weight. The otherwise proper citizen may avoid committing himself during a scene of community "nigger-baiting." A man considered a drunkard and a n'er-do-well by the white community may be exceedingly gentle or generous in his dealings with Negroes. Thus, in a society governed by codes and superficial patterns of judgment, the Negro allows the character to step out of his structured world into the chaos of man-to-man relationships. The consequent view of the white character to which the reader is privy is often more revealing than all of the other precisely conformist dialogue and action.

Obviously, in those rare novels when the Negro moves to the center of the stage, he alters the entire vision of the white-dominated South. The reader is suddenly placed in an alien position from which the whole vision seems as distorted as in a mannerist painting. The motives for actions seem confusing, the response to characters demands reconsideration of values, the whole mode of existence is altered. Unfortunately, too many of the Negro-centered novels retain the white point-of-view so that this reorientation is seldom demanded of the reader. But in those rare cases when we do enter into the life of the Southern Negro and see the world through his eyes, we find it an exciting and often an infuriating world.

As hero, he has the alternatives of any hero: he may fight violently, suffer deeply, escape, revolt, thrive, love, hate, and die either heroically, pathetically, or naturally. His values matter to the reader because they reflect the values of his author and of the society for which that author writes. Thus, when he measures life by a bank account or a coat of paint, we grieve at his limited goals, but the author may convince us that they are also society's goals. Usually, the goal of the Negro hero is simply survival—preferably with some shreds of human dignity, but dignity notwithstanding, survival anyway. Because this is a very real problem for the Negro, he has the potential of a truly tragic hero as modern characters seldom do. The modern author must contrive a situation that honestly deals with life-and-death decisions: an escaped murderer in the house, a prisoner of war hoping to escape, or a man contemplating suicide. For the Negro, the specter of death or castration is much nearer at hand.

Thus, aesthetically the Negro is invaluable to the Southern novelist. If he is central to the action, he can be lynched or threatened with lynching to serve in the climactic scene. If he is a friend of the key white character, he can precipitate the moment of truth when the white man must face up to the lynch mob or the illegitimate mulatto child or whatever, and act out the role of hero or villain. Because he is better informed than the white characters, he can frequently serve as the crux of the recognition scene. In more sophisticated novels, he can serve as the image that must be stripped of its mask to discover the reality and ambiguity of life. He may also serve as a symbol of self-hatred or of the search for identity. He is always useful for categorizing men as brutal or gentle, thoughtless or tactless. His mystery (symbolized by his color) can serve as a satisfying image of the mystery of human life and personality. His isolation can stand for everyman's isolation. His misery is the microcosm of human suffering; and his endurance is everyman's hope for the strength to endure and prevail. In short, he is one of the most valuable components of Southern fiction and one of the reasons for the superior quality of modern Southern literature.

The nineteenth-century South exploited the Negro economically; the twentieth-century South is learning to exploit him aesthetically.

NOTES

BIBLIOGRAPHY

INDEX

NOTES

CHAPTER 1

1. Howard Odum, *Rainbow Round My Shoulder* (Indianapolis, 1928), p. 211.
2. Sterling Brown *et al., The Negro Caravan* (New York, 1941), p. 3.
3. Sterling Brown, *The Negro in American Fiction* (Washington, D.C., 1937), p. 3.
4. Howard Odum, "Literature in the South: An Exchange of Views," in Louis D. Rubin, Jr. and Robert D. Jacobs (eds.), *Southern Renascence: The Literature of the Modern South,* (Baltimore, 1953), p. 83.
5. Hamilton Basso, *Cinnamon Seed* (New York, 1934), p. 74.
6. W.T. Couch, "The Negro in the South," in *Culture in the South* (Chapel Hill, 1934), p. 434.
7. *Ibid.*
8. James W. Silver, *Mississippi: The Closed Society* (New York, 1963), p. 84.
9. Charles Silberman, *Crisis in Black and White* (New York, 1964), p. 72.
10. Brown, *The Negro Caravan,* p. 3.
11. William Faulkner, "The Bear," in *Go Down, Moses* (New York, 1942), p. 294.
12. Ralph Ellison, *Shadow and Act* (New York, 1953), p. 44.
13. *Ibid.,* p. 83.

CHAPTER 2

1. Hugh M. Gloster, *Negro Voices in American Fiction* (Chapel Hill, 1948), p. 8.

2. Lillian Smith, *Killers of the Dream* (New York, 1949), p. 131.
3. Hodding Carter, *Winds of Fear* (New York, 1944), p. 195.
4. Irene C. Edmonds, "Faulkner and the Black Shadow, " in *Southern Renascence*, p. 192.
5. Cleanth Brooks, *William Faulkner: The Yoknapatawpha Country* (New Haven, 1963), p. 306.
6. *Ibid.,* p. 290.
7. *Ibid.,* p. 344.
8. Robert Penn Warren, *Brother to Dragons* (New York, 1953), p. 52.
9. Brown, *The Negro in American Fiction,* p. 170.
10. Stanley Elkins, *Slavery: A Problem in American Institutional and Intellectual Life* (New York, 1963), pp. 81-88.
11. Sterling Brown, *The Negro in American Fiction,* pp. 17-18.
12. *Ibid.,* p. 192.
13. Bernard Wolfe, "Uncle Remus and the Malevolent Rabbit," *Commentary,* July 1949, pp. 31-44.

CHAPTER 3

1. Ralph McGill, *The South and the Southerner* (Boston, 1959), p. 115.
2. Silberman, p. 94.
3. Eric Lincoln, "The Absent Father Haunts the Negro Family," *New York Times Magazine,* November 28, 1965, pp. 60, 172-73.
4. Ellison, *Shadow and Act,* pp. 85-86.
5. Howard Odum, *Rainbow Round My Shoulder,* p. 40.
6. Silberman, p. 188.
7. *Ibid.,* p. 119.
8. Odum, *Rainbow Round My Shoulder,* p. 299.

CHAPTER 4

1. John Dollard, *Caste and Class in a Southern Town* (New York, 1957), p. 327.

2. Smith, pp. 116-17.
3. Edward Kimbrough, *Night Fire* (New York, 1946), p. 155.
4. Smith, p. 117.
5. Harper Lee, *To Kill a Mockingbird* (New York, 1960), p. 206.

CHAPTER 5

1. Couch, "The Negro in the South," p. 468.
2. Sterling Brown, "Negro Characters as Seen by White Authors," *Journal of Negro Education,* II (April 1933), p. 201.
3. Gloster, p. 12.
4. Brown, *The Negro in American Fiction,* p. 12.
5. Sterling Brown, "Alas the Poor Mulatto," *Opportunity,* XI (March 1933), p. 91.
6. Edmonds, in Rubin, *Southern Renascence,* p. 196.

CHAPTER 6

1. Ellison, *Shadow and Act,* p. 37.
2. W.J. Cash, *The Mind of the South,* pp. 119-20.
3. *Ibid.,* p. 125.
4. Howard Odum, "Fears and Folkways," *The Nation,* vol. 133 (December 30, 1931), pp. 719-20.
5. Smith, p. 158.
6. *Time,* vol. 87 (April 1966), p. 47.
7. *PMLA,* vol. 73 (1958), pp. 155-66.

CHAPTER 7

1. John Bradbury, *Renaissance in the South* (Chapel Hill, 1963), p. 18.
2. Sterling Brown, "Negro Character as Seen by White Authors," *Journal of Negro Education,* II (April 1933), pp. 195-96.
3. Robert A. Bone, *The Negro Novel in America* (New Haven, 1958), p. 112.
4. Gloster, p. 198.

5. Record Wilson, *The Negro and the Communist Party* (Chapel Hill, 1951).
6. Richard Wright, "I Tried to Be a Communist," *Atlantic Monthly,* vol. 174 (August 1944), p. 62.
7. Bone, p. 152.
8. Bradbury, p. 18.
9. Silberman, p. 28.
10. Thomas Clark, *The Emerging South* (New York, 1961), pp. 182-83.
11. Bucklin Moon, ed., *Primer for White Folks* (Garden City, N. Y., 1945), p. 289.

CHAPTER 8

1. Bone, p. 12.
2. Gloster, p. 29.
3. *Ibid.,* p. 98.
4. Clark, p. 77.
5. Couch, "The Negro in the South," p. 472.
6. McGill, p. 175.
7. Silberman, p. 109.

CHAPTER 9

1. Jay B. Hubbell, *Southern Life in Fiction* (Athens, Ga., 1960).

BIBLIOGRAPHY

Adams, Edward C.L. *Congaree Sketches*. Chapel Hill: University of North Carolina Press, 1927.

Agee, James, and Walker Evans. *Now Let Us Praise Famous Men*. Boston: Houghton Mifflin Company, 1939.

Alexander, L.M. *Candy*. New York: Dodd, Mead and Company, 1934.

Anderson, Barbara. *Southbound*. New York: Farrar, Straus and Company, 1949.

Attaway, William. *Blood on the Forge*. Garden City, New York: Doubleday, Doran and Company, Inc., 1941.

Baldwin, James. *Notes of a Native Son*. New York: Bantam Books, 1955.

Basso, Hamilton. *Cinnamon Seed*. New York: Charles Scribner's Sons, 1934.

—————. *Courthouse Square*. New York: Charles Scribner's Sons, 1936.

Bone, Robert A. *The Negro Novel in America*. New Haven: Yale University Press, 1958.

Bradbury, John M. *Renaissance in the South*. Chapel Hill: University of North Carolina Press, 1963.

Brink, William and Louis Harris. *The Negro Revolution in America*. New York: Simon and Schuster, 1964.

Brooks, Cleanth. *William Faulkner: The Yoknapatawpha Country*. New Haven: Yale University Press, 1963.

Brown, Joe David. *Kings Go Forth*. New York: William Morrow and Company, 1956.

Brown, Sterling. "Alas the Poor Mulatto," *Opportunity*, XI (1933), 91.

——————. "Local Color or Interpretation," *Opportunity*, X (1932), 223.

——————, Arthur P. David, and Ulysses Lee (eds.). *The Negro Caravan*. New York: The Citadel Press, 1941.

Brown, Sterling. "Negro Character as Seen by White Authors," *Journal of Negro Education*, II (April 1933), 179-203.

——————. *The Negro in American Fiction*. Washington, D.C.: Associates in Negro Folk Education, 1937.

——————. "A New Trend," *Opportunity,* XI (February 1933), 56.

Butcher, Margaret Just. *The Negro in American Culture*. New York: The New American Library, 1957.

Caldwell, Erskine. *American Earth*. New York: Duell, Sloan and Pearce, 1946.

——————. *The Caldwell Caravan*. New York: World Publishing Company, 1946.

——————, *In Search of Bisco*. New York: Farrar, Straus and Giroux, 1965.

——————. *Place Called Estherville*. New York: Duell, Sloan and Pearce, 1949.

——————. *Trouble in July*. Boston: Little, Brown and Company, 1940.

Capote, Truman. *The Grass Harp*. New York: Random House, 1951.

Carmer, Carl. *Stars Fell on Alabama*. New York: The Literary Guild, 1934.

Carter, Hodding. *The Winds of Fear*. New York: Farrar and Rinehart, Inc., 1944.

Cash, W.J. *The Mind of the South*. New York: Knopf, 1941.

Cheney, Brainard. *This Is Adam.* New York: McDowell, Obolensky, 1958.

Clark, Thomas D. *The Emerging South.* New York: Oxford University Press, 1961.

Coker, Elizabeth Boatwright. *Daughter of Strangers.* New York: E.P. Dutton and Company, Inc., 1950.

Coleman, Lonnie. *Clara.* New York: E.P. Dutton and Company, Inc., 1952.

————. *Escape the Thunder.* New York: E.P. Dutton and Company, Inc., 1944.

Coleman, Richard. *Don't You Weep . . . Don't You Moan.* New York: The Macmillan Company, 1935.

Couch, W.T. (ed.). *Culture in the South.* Chapel Hill: University of North Carolina Press, 1934.

Creekmore, Hubert. *The Chain in the Heart.* New York: Random House, 1953.

Daniels, Lucy. *Caleb, My Son.* New York: J.B. Lippincott Company, 1956.

Davidson, Donald. *Southern Writers in the Modern World.* Athens, Georgia: University of Georgia Press, 1958.

Davis, Paxton. *Two Soldiers.* New York: Simon and Schuster, 1956.

Dixon, Thomas. *The Clansman: An Historical Romance of the Ku Klux Klan.* New York: Grosset and Dunlap, 1905.

————. *The Leopard's Spots: A Romance of the Ku Klux Klan.* New York: Grosset and Dunlap, 1905.

Dollard, John. *Caste and Class in a Southern Town.* New York: Doubleday-Anchor, 1957.

Ehle, John. *Move Over, Mountain.* New York: William Morrow and Company, 1957.

Elkins, Stanley M. *Slavery: A Problem in American Institutional and Intellectual Life.* New York: The Universal Library, 1963.

Ellison, Ralph. *Invisible Man*. New York: Random House, 1947.

──────. *Shadow and Act*. New York: Random House, 1953.

Faulkner, William. *Absalom! Absalom!* New York: Modern Library, 1951.

──────. *Big Woods*. New York: Random House, 1931.

──────. *Go Down, Moses*. New York: Random House, 1942.

──────. *The Hamlet*. New York: Random House, 1948.

──────. *Intruder in the Dust*. New York: Random House, 1931.

──────. *Light in August*. New York: Modern Library, 1932.

──────. *The Mansion*. New York: Random House, 1955.

──────. *Requiem for a Nun*. New York: Random House, 1950.

──────. *The Rievers: A Reminiscence*. New York: Random House, 1962.

──────. *Sartoris*. New York: Harcourt, Brace and Co., 1929.

──────. *The Sound and the Fury*. New York: Harcourt, Brace and Co., 1929.

──────. *The Unvanquished*. New York: Random House, 1934.

Feibleman, Peter S. *A Place Without Twilight*. New York: The World Publishing Company, 1957.

Flannagan, Roy. *Amber Satyr*. New York: Doubleday, Doran and Company, Inc., 1932.

Frank, Waldo. *Holiday*. New York: Boni and Liveright, 1923.

Furnas, J.C. *Goodbye to Uncle Tom*. New York: William Sloane Associates, 1956.

Gaither, Frances. *Follow the Drinking Gourd*. New York: The Macmillan Company, 1940.

──────. *The Red Cock Crows*. New York: The Macmillan Company, 1944.

Glasgow, Ellen. *Barren Ground*. New York: Sagamore, 1957.

——————. *In This Our Life*. New York: Doubleday, Doran and Company, Inc., 1932.

——————. *The Sheltered Life*. New York: Harcourt, Brace and Co., 1941.

——————. *Virginia*. Garden City, New York: Doubleday, Page and Company, 1913.

Gloster, Hugh M. *Negro Voices in American Fiction*. Chapel Hill: University of North Carolina Press, 1948.

Gordon, Arthur. *Reprisal*. New York: Simon and Schuster, 1950.

Gordon, Caroline. *The Forest of the South*. New York: Charles Scribner's Sons, 1945.

Gossett, Thomas F. *Race: The History of an Idea in America*. Dallas: Southern Methodist University Press, 1963.

Grau, Shirley Ann. *The Black Prince*. New York: Alfred A. Knopf, 1955.

——————. *The Keepers of the House*. New York: Alfred A. Knopf, 1964.

Green, Paul. *The Field God* and *In Abraham's Bosom*. New York: Robert M. McBride and Company, 1928.

——————. *Lonesome Road: Six Plays for the Negro Theatre*. New York: Robert M. McBride and Company, 1926.

Gross, Seymour L., and John Edward Hardy (eds.). *Images of the Negro in American Literature*. Chicago: University of Chicago Press, 1966.

Gwaltney, Francis Irby. *The Number of Our Days*. New York: Random House, 1959.

Hare, Nathan. *The Black Anglo-Saxons*. New York: Marzani and Munsell, Inc., 1965.

Henderson, George Wylie. *Ollie Miss*. New York: Frederick A. Stokes Company, 1935.

Hewlett, John. *Harlem Story*. New York: Prentice-Hall, Inc., 1948.

──────. *Wild Grape*. New York: McGraw-Hill Book Co., Inc., 1947.

Heyward, DuBose. *Mamba's Daughters*. New York: The Literary Guild, 1929.

──────. *Porgy*. New York: Grosset and Dunlap, 1925.

Hoffman, Fredrick J. *William Faulkner*. New York: Twayne Publishers, Inc., 1961.

Hubbell, Jay B. *Southern Life in Fiction*. Athens: University of Georgia Press, 1960.

Hurston, Zora Neale. *Seraph on the Suwanee*. New York: Charles Scribner's Sons, 1948.

──────. *Their Eyes Were Watching God*. Philadelphia: J.B. Lippincott Company, 1937.

Isaacs, Harold R. *The New World of Negro Americans*. New York: The John Day Company, 1963.

Johnson, Charlotte Payne. *Watching at the Window*. New York: The Bobbs-Merrill Company, Inc., 1955.

Johnson, Victor H. *The Horncasters*. New York: Greenberg, 1947.

Jones, Carter Brooke. *The White Band*. New York: Funk and Wagnalls Co., 1959.

Joseph, Donald. *Straw in the South Wind*. New York: The Macmillan Company, 1946.

Kelley, Welbourn. *Inchin' Along*. New York: William Morrow and Company, 1932.

Kiker, Douglas. *The Southerner*. New York: Rinehart and Company, Inc., 1957.

Killens, John Oliver. *And Then We Heard the Thunder*. New York: Alfred A. Knopf, 1963.

Kimbrough, Edward. *Night Fire*. New York: Rinehart and Company, Inc., 1946.

Kolb, Avery E. *Jigger Whitchet's War*. New York: Simon and Schuster, 1959.

Lee, Harper. *To Kill a Mockingbird*. New York: Popular Library, 1960.

Lincoln, Eric. "The Absent Father Haunts the Negro Family, " *New York Times Magazine*, November 28, 1965, pp. 60, 172-73.

Locke, Alain (ed.). *The New Negro: An Interpretation*. New York: Albert and Charles Boni, 1925.

Lowrey, Walter B. *Watch Night*. New York: Charles Scribner's Sons, 1953.

McCullers, Carson. *Clock Without Hands*. Boston: Houghton Mifflin Company, 1961.

––––––. *The Heart Is a Lonely Hunter*. Boston: Houghton Mifflin Company, 1940.

––––––. *The Member of the Wedding*. Boston: Houghton Mifflin Company, 1946.

McGill, Ralph Emerson. *The South and the Southerner*. Boston: Little, Brown and Company, 1959.

March, William. *Come in at the Door*. New York: Harrison Smith and Robert Haas, 1934.

Meade, Julian R. *The Back Door*. New York: Longmans, Green and Company, 1938.

Millen, Gilmore. *Sweet Man*. New York: The Viking Press, 1930.

Moon, Bucklin (ed.). *Primer for White Folks*. Garden City, New York: Doubleday, Doran and Company, Inc., 1945.

Morris, Willie (ed.). *The South Today*. New York: Harper and Row, 1965.

Myrdal, Gunnar. *An American Dilemma*. New York: Harper and Row, 1962.

O'Connor, Flannery. *Everything That Rises Must Converge*. New York: Farrar, Straus, and Giroux, 1965.

O'Connor, William Van. *The Tangled Fire of William Faulkner.* Minneapolis: University of Minnesota Press, 1954.

Odum, Howard W. *Folk, Region, and Society.* Chapel Hill: University of North Carolina Press, 1964.

—————. *Rainbow Round My Shoulder.* Indianapolis, Indiana: The Bobbs-Merrill Company, Publishers, 1928.

Page, Dorothy Myra. *Gathering Storm.* New York: International Publishers, 1932.

Page, Thomas Nelson. *In Old Virginia or Marse Chan and Other Stories.* New York: Charles Scribner's Sons, 1924 (orig. 1887).

Peterkin, Julia. *Black April.* New York: Grosset and Dunlap, 1927.

—————. *Bright Skin.* Indianapolis: The Bobbs-Merrill Company, 1932.

—————. *Scarlet Sister Mary.* Philadelphia: The Blackiston Company, 1928.

Pettigrew, Thomas F. *A Profile of the Negro American.* Princeton, New Jersey: D. Van Nostrand Company, Inc., 1964.

Pierce, Ovid Williams. *On a Lonesome Porch.* New York: Doubleday and Company, Inc., 1960.

—————. *The Plantation.* New York: Doubleday and Company, Inc., 1953.

Pope, Edith. *Colcorton.* New York: Charles Scribner's Sons, 1944.

Porteous, Clark. *South Wind Blows.* New York: A.A. Wyn, Publisher, 1948.

Reece, Byron Herbert. *The Hawk and the Sun.* New York: E.P. Dutton and Company, Inc., 1955.

Rogers, Lettie Hamlett. *Birthright.* New York: Simon and Schuster, 1957.

Rubin, Louis D., Jr., and Robert D. Jacobs (eds.). *Southern Renascence: The Literature of the Modern South.* Baltimore, Maryland: The Johns Hopkins Press, 1953.

Russell, William. *A Wind Is Rising*. New York: Charles Scribner's Sons, 1950.

Shriver, Donald W., Jr. (ed.). *The Unsilent South: Prophetic Preaching in Racial Crisis*. Richmond, Virginia: John Knox Press, 1965.

Silberman, Charles E. *Crisis in Black and White*. New York: Random House, 1964.

Silver, James W. *Mississippi: The Closed Society*. New York: Harcourt, Brace and World, Inc., 1963.

Smith, Lillian. *Killers of the Dream*. New York: W.W. Norton and Company, 1949.

——————. *Strange Fruit*. New York: Reynal and Hitchcock, 1944.

Spencer, Elizabeth. *Fire in the Morning*. New York: Dodd, Mead and Company, 1948.

——————. *The Voice at the Back Door*. New York: McGraw-Hill Book Company, 1948.

Stribling, T.S. *Birthright*. New York: The Century Company, 1922.

——————. *Bright Metal*. Garden City, New York: Doubleday, Doran and Company, Inc., 1928.

——————. *The Forge*. Garden City, New York: The Sun Dial Press, Inc., 1938.

——————. *The Store*. New York: Literary Guild, 1932.

——————. *Unfinished Cathedral*. Garden City, New York: Country Life Press, 1934.

Styron, William. *Confessions of Nat Turner*. New York: Random House, 1967.

——————. *Lie Down in Darkness*. New York: Bobbs-Merrill Company, Inc., 1951.

——————. *Set This House on Fire*. New York: Random House, 1959.

Tate, Allen. *The Fathers*. London: Eyre and Spottiswoode, 1938.

Toomer, Jean. *Cane*. New York: Boni and Liveright, 1923.

Turpin, Waters E. *O Canaan!* New York: Doubleday, Doran and Company, Inc., 1939.

——————. *These Low Grounds*. New York: Harper and Brothers, Publishers, 1937.

Warren, Robert Penn. *At Heaven's Gate*. New York: Random House, 1943.

——————. *Band of Angels*. New York: Random House, 1955.

——————. *Brother to Dragons*. New York: Random House, 1953.

——————. *The Circus in the Attic and Other Stories*. New York: Harcourt, Brace and Company, 1947.

——————. *Flood*. New York: Random House, 1963.

——————. *The Legacy of the Civil War*. New York: Random House, 1961.

——————. *Segregation: The Inner Conflict in the South*. New York: Random House, 1956.

——————(ed.). *A Southern Harvest*. Boston: Houghton Mifflin Company, 1937.

——————. *Who Speaks for the Negro?* New York: Random House, 1965.

——————. *Wilderness*. New York: Random House, 1961.

——————. *World Enough and Time*. New York: Random House, 1950.

Welty, Eudora. *A Curtain of Green and Other Stories*. New York: Harcourt, Brace and Company, 1936.

Westheimer, David. *Summer on the Water*. New York: The Macmillan Company, 1948.

Williams, John A. *Sissie*. New York: Farrar, Straus and Cudahy, 1963.

Wilson, John Walter. *High John the Conqueror.* New York: The Macmillan Company, 1948.

Wolfe, Thomas. *Look Homeward, Angel.* New York: The Modern Library, 1929.

Wood, Clement. *Nigger.* New York: E. P. Dutton and Company, 1922.

Wright, Richard. *Black Boy: A Record of Childhood and Youth.* New York: Harper and Brothers, 1937.

——————. *Eight Man.* New York: Avon Book Division, 1961.

——————. *The Long Dream.* Garden City, New York: Doubleday and Company, Inc., 1958.

——————. *Native Son.* New York: Harper and Brothers, Publishers, 1940.

——————. *12 Million Black Voices: A Folk History of the Negro in the United States.* New York: The Viking Press, 1941.

Young, Jefferson. *A Good Man.* New York: The Bobbs-Merrill Company, Inc., 1952.

Zinn, Howard. *The Southern Mystique.* New York: Alfred A. Knopf, 1964.

INDEX

Agee, James, 144

Agrarian reformers: *I'll Take My Stand*, 31

Akers, Arthur, 44

Alexander, Mrs. L. M.: her *Candy*, 84; on morals, 189; on music, 187; on new Negro, 147; as example of primitivist, 125, 126

American Stuff, 127

Amos and Andy: as examples of comic Negro, 21, 44

Anderson, Barbara: *Southbound*, 65; color snobbery, 89; doctors, 155; on return South, 163

Archetypes: as modern trend, 17

Aristocrats, 151, 182, 195

Attaway, William: mentioned, 127, 137, 144; his *Blood on the Forge*, 121, 180; on lynching, 108; on unions, 134, 135

Audience for Southern literature, 178, 181

Babbitt, black: mentioned, 143; related to black sharecropper, 140

Baldwin, James: mentioned, 19, 79, 174, 180; on religion, 189, 190; on sex-envy, 61

Barr, Caroline, 32, 34

Basso, Hamilton: mentioned, 19, 21; his *Cinnamon Seed*, 76, 100; his *Courthouse Square*, 100; on violence, 110; on educated Negroes, 155

Beating scenes, 53, 54

Beauty: Negro v. white ideals of, 84, 101

Bontemps, Arna, 127

Bradford, Roark: mentioned, 44, 122; his "Cold Death," 32, 33; his *Old Man Adam*, 33

Brooks, Cleanth: on "blood," 192; on Dilsey, 34—35

Brown, Joe David, 99—100

Brown, Sterling: mentioned, 15, 21, 29, 31, 43, 44, 86; on stereotypes, 194; on the brute Negro, 60; on the exotic primitive, 123, 127

Brown, W. W., 150

Brute Negro: mentioned, 29, 80, 81, 82, 86, 92, 171, 178, 194; alterations in stereotype, 188; and lynching, 105; and Nat Turner, 173, 193; and the new Negro, 167, 168, 169, 175

Businessmen, black, 142, 143

Bynner, Witter, 169

Cable, George W.: his *The Grandissimes*, 87

Caldwell, Erskine: mentioned, 46; his *In Search of Bisco*, 65, 77, 179; his *A Place Called Estherville*, 83; his *Tobacco Road*, 37; on lynching, 113, 116; on peonage, 142; his sharecropper stories, 138—39

Capitalism: and *Invisible Man*, 130

Capote, Truman, 18, 182

Carter, Hodding: mentioned, 172; his *Winds of Fear*, law officers in, 109; leaders in, 170—71; teacher in, 161; preacher in, 159; picture of Uncle Tom character, 45

Cash, W. J.: mentioned, 181; on vio-